D1484342

神様の次に大切なものは海賊デス

JAPANESE MADE FUNNY

神様の次に大切なものは海賊デス

ガイジンのファニーなニホンゴ大全集

JAPANESE MADE FUNNY

Gaijin Bloops in Nihongo

トム・ディラン[著]
アンディ・バーガー[イラスト]
渡辺ミナ子[日本語訳]

by Tom Dillon

Illustrations by Andrew Boerger

Translation by Watanabe Minako

THE EAST PUBLICATIONS, INC.

© 2001 The East Publications, Inc.
All rights reserved
The East Publications, Inc.
Mamiana Arc Bldg., 1F
2-1 Higashi-Azabu 3,
Minato-ku
Tokyo, Japan
http://www.theeast.co.jp

Second printing 2002

Book design by Akira Ikeda

Printed in Japan

ISBN 4-915645-21-5

お買い上げの「バイリンガル・コミックス」のタイトルをお書きください。

b　ご住所　　　　　　　　　　　　　〒□□□-□□□□

c　お名前　　　　　　　　　　d　年齢　（　　　）歳

　　　　　　　　　　　　　　　e　性別　1 男性　2 女性

f　ご職業　1 大学生　2 短大生　3 高校生　4 中学生　5 各種学校生
　　　　　6 教職員　7 公務員　8 会社員(事務系)　9 会社員(技術系)　10 会社役員
　　　　　11 研究職　12 自由業　13 サービス業　14 商工従事　15 自営業　16 農林漁業
　　　　　17 主婦　18 家事手伝い　19 無職　20 その他(　　　　　　　　　　　)

g　この「バイリンガル・コミックス」をお選びいただいた理
　　由は何ですか。
　　　1 このコミックスのファンだから
　　　2 英語(英会話)の勉強になると思ったから
　　　3 趣味、娯楽のため
　　　4 その他(　　　　　　　　　　　　　　　　　　　　　)

h　この「バイリンガル・コミックス」を何で（どこで）お知
　　りになりましたか。

i　「バイリンガル・コミックス」で読みたいマンガ（日本・海
　　外）をあげてください。

j　どんなコミックスのノベルス（小説版）を英語で読みたい
　　ですか。

k　「講談社英語文庫」「講談社ルビー・ブックス」「講談社バイ
　　リンガル・ブックス」をご存じですか。ご存じでしたら、
　　読みたいタイトルをお教えください。

ご協力ありがとうございました。

1 1 2 - 8 7 9 0

東京都文京区音羽一丁目

十七番十四号

講談社

インターナショナル

講談社バイリンガル・コミックス

愛読者カード係　　行

料金受取人払

小石川局承認

3049

差出有効期間
平成13年8月
5日まで

ɑ. 本書と、この「バイリンガル・コミックス」シリーズについ
て、お気づきの点、ご感想などをお教えください。(内容、体裁、
値段などについても、ご意見をお待ちしています)

目次

contents

本書のために言い間違いの素材を提供して下さった方々に御礼を申し上げたいのだが、そうなると私は日本で出会った外国人のほとんど全員に感謝しなければならないような気がしている。というのも、一度も言い間違いをしたことのない外国人などひとりもいないからである。日本に長く住んでいるおかげで、私は外国人の言い間違いをずいぶん沢山耳にしてきたが、それは幸運なことだったと今は実感している。

　私は次の3つのネタ元に特に感謝したい。まずウィリアム・ウッド氏とその著書 "Let's Challenge the Japanese Language" に。この本の中でウッド氏は伝説的な言い間違いの数例を取り上げておられる。2番目に、在日外国人婦人協会の皆様に感謝する。東京で行われた同協会の2001年の例会の席では、大勢の会員の方々が、親切にも、それぞれがいちばん恥ずかしい思いをされた逸話を披露して下さった。そして「漫画人Mangajin」にも感謝したい。現在休刊中だが、興味深い雑誌で、言い間違いの連載コラムを毎月掲載していた。もう1人、国際基督教大学のジョージ・ビデル博士にも本書の発音の手引きの中の誤りをチェックして下さったことに対して御礼を申し上げたい。

　もちろん、自分のした言い間違いを寄稿して下さった方も大勢いる。これらの個人の皆様にも謝意を表したい。と同時に、彼ら/彼女らの未来の言い間違いがさほど大きなドジにはならないことを望みたい。

　しかしながら、私にとってもっとも安定した言い間違いの供給源は、おそらく私自身の口であった。本書に収載した言い間違いのうち、私自身が犯したものは幾つあるのか、それは申し上げかねる。ただし、その数は決して少なくはない。ということはつまり、もし私が本書の続編を書くとしても、その際もやはり一番の頼みの綱は私自身ということになりそうである。

トム・ディラン

東京にて，2001年10月

神様の次に大切なものは海賊デス

IN acknowledging my blooper sources I feel I should give a big thank you to almost every foreigner I've met in Japan. For there is not a single gaijin who has not made his or her share of language blunders. I just feel fortunate to have been around long enough to hear a fair amount of these.

I would also like to thank three specific sources: William Wood and his book, *Let's Challenge the Japanese Language,* which presents several legendary bloopers; The Association of Foreign Wives in Japan, many members of which were kind enough to relate their most embarrassing anecdotes at their 2001 annual convention in Tokyo; and *Mangajin* magazine, a swell publication, now defunct, which used to print a monthly blooper column. I also want to thank Dr. George Bedell of International Christian University for shooing the bugs from the Guide to Pronunciation.

There are, of course, many people who contributed their personal bloopers and to these individuals I offer my gratitude, as well as my hopes that all their future bloops be little ones.

Perhaps, however, my most consistent blooper source has been my own mouth. I refuse to say how many of the enclosed word bobbles belong to me, but the number is not small. Meaning, I suppose, that I am my own best hope for a sequel.

TOM DILLON
Tokyo
October 2001

次頁から、外国人読者のために、日本語の発音に関する基
本的な説明を行います。
日本人読者にとっては不要と思われるため、日本語訳は省
略致しました。ご諒承下さい。

編集部

JAPANESE terms in this book generally follow the Hepburn

Romanization system. Knowing how words in this system are pronounced may also provide insights as to how many bloops happen.

Of course a foreigner having just blooped needs to know this in the same way a doctor needs to do an autopsy on a shark victim. With half the body still in the animal's mouth, determining the cause of death seems superfluous.

So it goes with bloopers. All that matters with most learners is that they have been mangled by that slippery fish of the communicative seas—the Japanese language.

The idea then is not to autopsy errors past, but rather to avoid new ones. Thus, it may be best to think of the following guide as a sort of linguistic shark repellent. Keep it with you when you enter the water.

Vowel Sounds

Japan has only five vowel sounds and these are represented in Roman script by the letters a, i, u, e and o. This may seem comfortably familiar to many Western learners who had grammar school teachers pound into their heads that the English vowels were a, e, i, o, u...and sometimes y.

Yet, when Japanese grammar school teachers say there are only five vowels they really mean it. With English, while vowels are represented with only five letters (and sometimes y), the number of different sounds these letters can produce is prodigious.

Think of "cut," "cute," "curt" and "cuckoo," for example. The "u" sound is different in each case. In fact, linguists have identified oodles of English vowels and diphthongs, with the final number reaching into the dozens, depending on exactly which linguist you trust. Enough, anyhow, to drive learners of English cuckoo—no matter how you pronounce it.

Japanese, though, sticks to its five vowel sounds. Stresses are not as heavy as those in English and even unstressed syllables have vowels that are squeakingly

神様の次に大切なものは海賊デス

precise. Again, this is unlike English, which tends to present stressed vowels on a plate and leave the rest on a guttural cutting board. This butchered, all pervasive sound is otherwise known as the "schwa," or that lower case "e" that's been spun around backwards.

For example, in the four-syllable English word "speed-ometer" only the stressed second syllable presents the vowel sound clearly. The remaining vowels are "schwaed."

So the first clue to handling Japanese pronunciation properly is to keep the vowels in order. Don't mix them up and don't reduce them to the dull-toned schwa. And if they're in Roman script don't read them like they were English! For while the vowels might be printed as in English, each letter stands for a very different sound. Note the following key:

Romanized vowel	Actual sound
a	This is pronounced as the vowel in "hot." Never as the "a" in "hat" and never as the "a" in hate. Think instead of what grammar school teachers used to call the "short o."
i	This is pronounced as the "ee" in "whee!" Don't draw the vowel out too long as foreigners are wont to do. Keep

	your reins tight and pull the sound up sharp. In other words, whoa your whee.
u	Remember that old song by The Five Stairsteps, "O-o-h child?" You don't? Too bad, for that's this sound—"o-o-h"—or similar to the vowel in "tune" or "moon."
e	Now we have the vowel sound as in "hate," "bait," "great" or "freight," only the sound that is spelled in so many ways in English is here represented by just one letter. Whoa this sound too.
o	Think "long o," the same "o" sound as in "Oh...Oklahoma, where the wind goes skipping down the plain!"

No matter what the consonants that precede them, if you can hang on to just these five sounds, you will go far in ridding yourself of pronunciation bloopers.

神様の次に大切なものは海賊デス

CONSONANTS

Compared with vowels, Romanized Japanese consonants present very few troubles, especially if you take care to pronounce them all clearly. Here are a few of the more unique consonants, the ones most likely to trip you up.

Some Japanese words begin with a tsu syllable, with lots of English words having this "ts" combination at the end (Example: lots)—but none at the beginning. The initial tsu sound is therefore not so hard; it just takes practice.

The Japanese r sound is a bit harder and is sometimes described as being halfway between an English l and r. Linguists might throw up over such an explanation, so don't tell them and instead concentrate on making the sound.

To make the Japanese r, cross all your fingers and then move your tongue forward in a flapping motion, just grazing the roof of your mouth. Put most of your emphasis on the tongue part and keep practicing.

The Japanese g when combined with a—in other words ga—takes on a nasal tone that English g's do not have. Neither is this Japanese g as hard and mean as an initial English g, say as in how an American would pronounce "Godzilla." Make this soft ga by arching the back of your tongue against the roof of you mouth and then pronouncing through your nose. Do it well and it may sound like a duck call. So practice inside.

All Japanese words end with a vowel with one exception, those ending with a final n. The Japanese final n is similar to an English "n"—only it is different. The English "n" is most often produced by placing the tongue on the ridge behind the upper teeth. The Japanese final n is formed by arching the back of the tongue up against the roof of the mouth. Think of it as a ga with no vowel and no g. Indeed, in isolation, the Japanese n sounds somewhat like a soft, half-stifled gulp.

Sounds in Succession

So far, so good, but of course it can't be this easy. The Japanese language has a wrinkle written English does not. That being: the same consonant or vowel symbol appearing in succession will signify a different pronunciciation of the word.

In English spelling, such consecutive consonants often have no effect on pronunciation. The words "but" and "butt," for instance, have different meanings, but are pronounced exactly the same.

Not so in Japanese, where all such consonants are pronounced. Take the words, **kite** and **kitte**, for example.

Kite—at least in one reading of Chinese characters—means to come. Kitte means "stamp," as in what you affix to an envelope. To a Japanese these words sound totally different and any foreigner who does not say the *t* twice when asking for stamps—as in kit-te—is instead

神様の次に大切なものは海賊デス

telling the postal worker to please come.

This is also true when the same vowel appears in succession. Kiite is a word meaning to hear. The i vowel must be said twice, for if not the word is no different than kite— to come, per above. In this case, instead of asking for stamps you would be telling the postal worker to please listen.

The consecutive vowel sounds that vex foreigners most are oo and o with a u, two combinations that essentially sound the same. Yet, to Japanese ears they are both different from a single o. In English, whether we say "open" or "OHpen" makes no difference. The word is still the same. But in Japanese such a change result in a different meaning. Take "Gotoh" and "gohtoh," for example—both of which will sound the same to a beginning learner. The first is a fairly common family name; the second is a thief.

Taking this into consideration, it's a wonder foreigners don't bloop even more often!

More than this, the confusion caused between how an English speaker sees Romanized vowels and consonants and the actual sounds those letters represent is a good reason to skip Roman script altogether when learning Japanese. Japanese scripts may be difficult, but one thing is certain: They will keep your pronunciation straight.

Or rather straighter.

For everyone bloops sometimes. But the only way to get over it is to stay in the water...and keep trying.

――――――――――

In the text, the symbol ^ indicates an elongated vowel in Japanese.

神様の次に大切なものは海賊デス

陽気で自信家のアメリカ人デイブ（仮名）が転勤で日本に来てもう一年が経つ。日本語もだいぶうまくなった。(少なくとも本人はそのつもり)。ある日デパートに買物に行ったデイブは、紳士服売場でワイシャツを買うことにした。売場の女店員に明るく大きな声で話しかけた。「すいませーん、ワイセツくださーい！」。

この手の言葉の失敗は外国人なら誰にでもあるものだ。それはときには痛ましい悲劇を生み、ときには抱腹絶倒の喜劇になる。

おそらく世界中で日本人ほど失敗を好む民族も珍しいだろう。これは、日本社会では形式や秩序がとても重視されているので、その分そうした秩序が突然崩壊するのを見るときに感じる喜びも大きいからかも知れない。

実際、日本はあらゆる種類の失敗の花園となっている。テレビ番組のNGシーン、各家庭で作られる自分たち家族のドジをおさめたビデオ、また野球やサッカーの珍プレイなどが日本中で咲き乱れ、大きな人気を呼んでいる。また日本の政治家の失言は国際的におなじみだが、日本人は表向きはそれを批判しつつ、実はそれを楽しみにしている。

しかし言葉のしくじりの汲めども尽きぬ泉といえば、なんといっても、子供と外国人である。本書では後者の活躍に焦点を絞った。外国人の言い間違いは子供の言い間違いほど微笑ましくないことも多い。しかし破壊力の点では決して子供にヒケをとらない。理性的であることを暗黙のうちに期待されている分だけ、外国人は無意識の喜劇役者として有利なのである。

本書におさめた外国人による日本語の言い間違いは１００例を越えるが、その収集方法はさほど学術的とは言

神様の次に大切なものは海賊デス

えない。その大半は著者の友人や知り合いから、ほんの数か月の間に聞き集めたものである。これらの話のいくつかは、本文でもことわっているが、他のメディアですでに紹介された話を脚色したものである。

たぶん本書の読者は「この話はみんな本当にあった話なのか？」という疑問を感じるに違いない。答えはイエス。ただし、いくつかの言い間違いに関しては、本来の状況とは多少違った背景のもとで起こった話のようにアレンジしてある。しかし大部分は実話そのままである。

本書で紹介する言い間違いの数々は４つのグループに分かれて登場する。「Where Are Your Breasts?」は質問や依頼に関する言い間違いをまとめたもの、「The Water's Full of Fried Chicken」は感想や告白を扱った章、「Give Up Your Wife and Heaven is Yours!」は誤った説明や表現を集めたもの、そして最後の「The Little Elephant's Penis」では聞き違いや読み違い、そしていずれの部類にも入らない失敗を取り上げている。

最後にひとつ警告を。本書の取材をしているとき、数人が語ってくれたそれぞれの言い間違いが偶然にも同じだった。言いかえれば、大勢の人々がまったく同じ間違いをおかしているということである。これはつまり、もし注意しないと、歴史同様に失敗も繰り返す傾向があるということだろう。とはいっても、歴史と言葉のしくじりは違う。歴史を読めば人は泣けてくる。言葉のしくじりは人に思わず笑い声をあげさせる。願わくば神よ、言い間違いに厚き御加護のあらんことを。

(編集部註：日本語のまえがきは英文のintroductionと内容が異なります)。

ADVENTURES IN BLOOPERLAND

ONCE upon a time a Japanese boy named Taro spent the night with a U.S. family in rural Ohio. It was the first stop on his high school group's tour of the United States.

Not the talkative sort, even in Japanese, Taro had nonetheless been coached by his teachers not to be shy in an American home. It wasn't the American way to be retiring and quiet, he was told. If he wanted something or he had something to say, he should speak right out.

So Taro, a large boy with a pouting lower lip and faltering English, pressed both his lip and his language skills to new limits. He cleared his throat and announced...

"I'm angry."

His jovial hosts were stunned to silence. The boy sat there on the sofa like a stone. What had they done to offend him?

One by one they dropped down around Taro, their eyes wired with worry. "What's wrong," his host mother begged.

"I'm angry," Taro said again, this time with more emphasis. He glanced from face to anxious face.

"But why!?" They wanted to know. With not one of the host family able to speak a single word of Japanese.

"Why?" Taro thought. "Why? What kind of a question was that?"

He didn't know enough English to answer. So he just said, "I am very angry."

Now his host mother began to sniffle. She had been so eager to show Taro American hospitality. Now—somehow—she and the family must have brought insult to his unfathomable oriental ways.

"Whatever we've done," she cried, "we're sorry!"

As Taro blinked with bewilderment, his host father hurriedly called the home where the Japanese teacher had lodged.

"I don't know, I don't know," the father sputtered into the phone. "The kid just keeps saying he's angry."

The receiver was passed to Taro. He spoke to the teacher briefly in guttural Japanese and then handed the device back to the father— who listened for several seconds, thanked the teacher kindly and set down the phone.

"Um..." the father began, his family holding their breath with concern. "The boy didn't mean 'angry.' " The father smiled. "He meant...'hungry.' "

There came a pause, as the looks of concern melted away. Then came grins. Then comes roars of laughter.

Taro too sat with his first American smile, albeit a plastic one. Whatever the wild joke was, he didn't get it.

Not that it mattered. All he wanted was a bite to eat.

Hungry young Taro had done what language learners do all over the world.

He blooped.

神様の次に大切なものは海賊デス

Lexical goofs, pronunciation flubs, hearing blunders... Anyone who has skated out to try a new language has at sometime or other crashed. Often these impacts are painful and other times humiliating. Yet, they can also be hilarious.

As well as instructional. For you can bet that Taro never confused "hungry" and "angry" again.

And that, talkative or not, he will treasure the story of his improbable word bungle for the rest of his life.

Language learning bloops—and all the wider family of both physical and speech-related gaffes—mollify the soul. They cross cultures. They span age gaps. For in stumbling our way through life, we all realize that somehow, someway each person is but a blooper waiting to happen. If not today, tomorrow. If not tomorrow, the day after. Therefore, to watch somebody else bend over and split their pants, tangle their lines in a stage play or knock a golf ball off an oak tree right back into their own groin presses a familiar button inside us all.

Because we know that there but for the grace of God go we...and a happy part of the humor comes in this time having the victim be someone else.

Ergo bloopers transcend. Universal in scope, they knot the human race together. And perhaps even more than that.

For take a gander at an okapi. Or a duck-billed platypus. Or a chihuahua. Sometimes, it can seem, even the Creator will bloop.

Yet while bloopers may thus link man with life eternal, the term itself is not so old. Legend says an announcer named Kermitt Schaeffer brought the word to life with a series of radio recordings in the mid-1940's. But since radio broadcasts in those days were virtually all live, most of Schaeffer's "recorded" bloops were either re-creations or out-and-out fakes.

The source of the term is also fuzzy. Schaeffer may have bred the word from the yowl of an oscillating radio frequency or from the name of a cheap hit in baseball, one resulting when a mighty swing serves but to boink the ball into the outfield.

Either way, within a few years of Schaeffer's best-selling albums, the word "blooper" had earned a place in both the dictionary and people's hearts. Popular forms include...

Fumbled out-takes from film, TV and radio... In the computer-animation feature *A Bug's Life*, for example, Disney Pixar even tossed in a section of bogus cartoon bloopers which showed the film's animated characters gumming their lines. Meanwhile, home video bloopers have pratfallen their way into prime time stardom around the globe.

Recorded malapropisms from celebrities... "A person can observe a lot just by watching," once noted New York Yankee catcher Yogi Berra. Supposedly he later repeated himself and then exclaimed, "Why, it's like deja vu all over again!"

神様の次に大切なものは海賊デス

Printed errors from books, newspapers and maga-
zines... Or even church bulletins, one of which announced, "Don't let worry kill you! Have the church help
instead!" In the same category, copies of real-life student
bloopers now swamp the Internet. "The Gorgons were
like women," writes one student, "Only more terrible."

Perhaps no nation on earth loves bloopers as much
as the Japanese. This may be because Japanese society
puts so much emphasis on form and order that to see
that order suddenly snap cracks the national funny
bone.

The Japanese are also famous for laughing when embarrassed, a cultural trait that many find embarrassing—
making them laugh even more.

Consequently Japan is a haven for bloopers of all sorts.
Local airwaves are asplash with shows of sloppy out-
takes, home-video goofs and baseball and soccer howl-
ers. Not to mention the regular verbal bobbles of Japanese politicians, a Japanese blooper institution all in itself.

Another blooper reservoir lies in the tricky abyss of
the Japanese language.

Replete with a vast lexicon and thorned with various
levels of polite speech, the language sits as ripe for slip-
ups as a well-positioned banana peel on a shadowy stairwell, with many native speakers eager to admit that they
themselves cannot handle their own tongue. While this
admission may be linguistic hogwash—as the people who

insist such are of course perfectly fluent—it does speak to the perceived complexity of the language and, once again, to the national obsession with form.

Which brings us back to language learners. This time not Japanese students trying their tender English, but rather foreigners—or **gaijin** as they are called in Japan—taking their chances with confounded **Nihongo**.

Talk about a blooper formula. Take one foreigner from Indo-European stock, perhaps one with a pronunciation system similar to that of American English, where the vowels of non-stressed syllables are regularly reduced to a clunky "schwa." Plug in this enormous and befuddling lexicon. Then add the fact that vowel sounds in Japanese are always crystal clear and that the meaning of words can change dramatically with the alteration of a single sound.

What we are left with might be called the foreigner's bane. For those not raised here, the Japanese language sits as a trapdoor forever ready to spring. Only the diligent—and the lucky—can escape.

Making this worse is that many Japanese find foreigners incomprehensible anyway. So that when an outsider makes a statement a trifle bizarre, some listeners might not trace the strangeness to a language snarl and merely conclude that life abroad is odd indeed.

And so, given both the difficulty of the language and the expectations of the listeners, foreign speakers do produce some notable mistakes. A wellspring of them, in fact.

神様の次に大切なものは海賊デス

Some of these flubs are silly, others are embarrassing and still others are outright incredible. Most act as but minor snags in communication; yet others stop that communication cold. The zaniest though nudge the conversation onto separate tracks, where the dialog gains an impish double meaning.

Following is a collection of over a hundred Japanese language bloopers, gathered rather unscientifically, mostly from friends and acquaintances, over a period of just a few months. Some of these stories possess almost mythical status, known to virtually every language learner in the land. A few have also been adapted from other media sources, as noted in the text.

Whatever, the best of these bloopers have been carefully tinkered into contexts of distinct double entendre, in which both speaker and listener go tooting down opposite tracks—blissfully unaware that they are in Blooperland until it is too, too late.

Are all these bloopers genuine? Did someone really say them?

With some necessary qualification...yes. For a small minority of the enclosed misfires have been more "suggested" than related—as being "**gaijin**-makeable" errors—and several more have been encased in contexts fairly different from the original blip.

Yet, for the fatter part of reality, these are true stories. The people who made them know.

Animal bloopers, food bloopers, boy-girl bloopers,

church bloopers and more, the most difficult task came in carving the material into some reasonable sense of order—an endeavor which shows bloopers have no order. They're just fun.

Still, as books string together better in parts, the bloopers presented here will sail your way grouped in four sections: "Where Are Your Breasts?" a unit on gaijin questions and requests; "The Water's Full of Fried Chicken," a chapter on observations and confessions; "Give Up Your Wives and Heaven Is Yours," a collection of misguided explanations and presentations; and last, "The Little Elephant's Penis," hearing and reading based goofs, plus a few other assorted bloops that defy all categorization.

One final word of caution. In research for this book, several individuals related identical boo-boos. In other words, numerous people had committed the exact same mistake. Sort of like deja vu all over again.

Meaning if you're not careful, just like history, bloopers tend to repeat themselves.

The difference being with history you read it and weep; with bloopers you read them and whoop.

Here they are. Happy blooping.

神様の次に大切なものは海賊デス

あなたのオチチは
どこですか？
質問や依頼の言い間違い

■■■■■■■■ 日本 にやってきた外国人は、質問をせずに
この国で生き延びていくことはできない。

　たとえばこんな風に彼らはたずねる。「この電車に乗れ
ばいいんですか？」「切符を買ったんですが、これで大丈夫
でしょうか？」「どのくらいしたら、電車を降りればいいん
ですか？」「一体どうしてこの電車は、どこにも停まらない
んでしょう？」「なぜこの電車には私しか乗ってないんで
しょうか？」

　以下に紹介するのは、ガイジンがたずねた他のいくつか
の質問の例である。どれもおかしな質問ばかりで、言い間
違いワンダーランドならではの良い質問である。

神様の次に大切なものは海賊デス

WHERE ARE YOUR BREASTS?

And other blooped questions and requests

NO guest can survive long in Japan without asking questions.

A la: Is this my train? Did I buy the right ticket? How soon do I get off? Why the hell doesn't the damn thing ever stop? And how come I'm the only one on board?

Following are a few other gaijin queries. This time, of the fractured variety, straight from Blooperland.

　　　　　　　　ある真夜中のこと、ひとりの外国人女性が
街角の食料品店に大急ぎで入って行った。その小さな店に
は、レジにしわくちゃのおじいさんがいるだけで、他にだ
れもいなかった。その女性は店内の商品棚に目をやりなが
ら、狭い通路を足早に行ったり来たりした。さっと店内を
一巡すると、向きをかえて店内を再び入念に見て回った。
彼女の顔は落胆でひきつった。

　「何かお探しですか？」。じいさんが言った。

　「ええ、探しています…」。女性はまずまずの日本語を話
した。だが、次に彼女が言った言葉は、まったく通じな
かった。

　「コヤシはないんですか？」。

　肥やし！？ じいさんは呆然と女性を見つめた。「一体何
で肥やしなど欲しいのだろう。それに何だってこの店でそ
んな物を探しているのか」と、彼は心の中でつぶやいた。
この外国人女性が言おうとしていたのは「もやし」だった
ことなど、じいさんにはわかるはずもなかった。女性の方
も自分の言い間違いに気づかず、「肥やし」と「もやし」と
ではまるで大違いということを知らなかった。

　「いやあ、申し訳ないですが、うちでは肥やしは扱って
いないですなあ」。

　「あら、ないんですか？ でもアメリカじゃ、コヤシを缶
詰で売ってるのをときどき見ますけど」。女性は指でその
缶詰の形を作ってみせた。「日本にはコヤシの缶詰はない
んですか？」。

　店主は首を振った。アメリカってなんておかしな国だ
ろう、と思いながら。

　「ええ、日本では肥やしを缶詰にするなんてことはまず

神様の次に大切なものは海賊デス

IN mid-evening a foreign woman rushes into the corner grocery store. Except for the wrinkled granddad behind the register, the tiny shop is empty.

The woman swings up and down the crimped aisles, sweeping each shelf with her eyes. She glides through once and then bends around and combs the store again. Her face pinches with frustration.

"Can I help you?" asks the man.

"Yes, yes you can... " The woman speaks passable Japanese, but what she says next will not pass at all.

"Don't you have any **koyashi**?"

koyashi

Koyashi?!! The man gapes at the woman, thinking: "Why in the world does she want **koyashi**!? And why is she looking for it here?"

Not guessing that what the foreign lady really means is **moyashi**—or "bean sprouts." Neither does the woman realize she has blooped and that **koyashi** has a very different meaning...manure.

moyashi

"No, I'm afraid we don't carry manure."

"Oh you don't? But in the States we sometimes sell it in cans." The woman makes the shape with her fingers. "Japanese don't do that?"

The storekeeper shakes his head. How weird America is, he thinks.

"No, we never can manure. Ours is always fresh. But — to be honest—I don't know any place that sells it."

The woman nods and confesses, "Every store I go to says the same thing," then steps for the door.

ありませんな。こちらじゃいつも新鮮なものを使いますから。でも...正直なところ...わたしは肥やしを売っているような店なんてひとつも知りませんが」。

　女性はうなずいて言った。「どの店に行っても同じことを言われました」。そう言って、彼女はドアの方へ歩いた。

　「なぜ肥やしが欲しいんですか？」。店主が女性に言った。

　女性は振り返り、当惑した面持ちでじいさんの方をちらりと見た。「なぜって...サラダにのせるためですよ。それ以外に考えられますか？」。

さて、場面はあるハイスクール——たまたまこの場合は女子校——へと変わる。新任の若いガイジン教師が立って、初めての出欠をとろうとしていた。少女たちは大した理由がなくても笑いこけるのだが、教師がとんでもない言い間違いをすれば、彼女たちは床にころげんばかりになることもある。

　この教師——ローエルと呼ぶことにしよう——は少女たちを下の名前で呼ぶことにした。ユミコ、ナオコ、マユミ...点呼は順調に進んだ。Ｊで始まるある名前に行き当たるまでは。その名前を呼ぶ段になると、さまざまな国を旅した経験のあるローエルは思わず自分が今何語を話しているのかを忘れてしまい、Ｊを発音せずにその名を言ってしまった。それがまずかった。その名前はジュンコだったから。「ウンコ？ウンコはいますか？」。クラス全員が爆笑した。

　ローエルには何がおかしいのかさっぱりわからなかった。だが、彼は返事をしてもらう必要があった。「ウンコはどこですか？」。

神様の次に大切なものは海賊デス

"Why do you want it?" the man calls.

She squints back with a puzzled eye. "Why...to put on salad. What else?"

NOW we move to a high school—in this case an all girls' school—where a young gaijin teacher stands taking roll for the very first time. The girls don't need much reason to giggle and when their teacher bloops big-time they can hardly keep from falling on the floor.

This man—let's call him Lowell—decides to call the girls by their first names. Yumiko, Naoko, Mayumi...everything goes fine until he hits a name starting with the letter "J." At which point the well-traveled Lowell forgets what language he's in and pronounces the name with the "J" silent. Which was unfortunate, for the name was **Junko**.

"**Unko**? Is **Unko** here?"

The class blows up with laughter. For **unko** is a common word for something you never want to step in, not even verbally. The list of euphemisms is long, but all smell bad. Perhaps the mildest term is "poop."

Junko

unko

　少女たちはあまりにも笑いこけたものだから、のどがつまらないように手で引っ張らなければならなかった。

　「ウンコは欠席ですか？本当に？」。

　ついに前列の少女が手をあげた。笑いすぎたために脇腹がひどく痛くて、彼女には自分の腕がすごく重く感じられた。

　「ああ、あなたがウンコですね」。ローエルは明るくほほえんだ。「あなたじゃないかなと思っていたんですよ！あなたはウンコという名に似つかわしい顔をしていますからね」。

　この男性はのちに日本人女性と結婚したが、読者のみなさんは彼の妻の名前を容易に想像できることだろう。噂によれば、彼は結婚の誓約でもドジを踏んだらしい。

　「私は汝を――ウンコを――愛、名誉、そして安らぎへと導くことを誓います...」。

ウンコ、肥やし等の日本語は、上述の例に見られるように、ガイジンにとってあらゆる種類の問題をもたらす。特にウンコはおそらくいちばん危険な言葉かもしれない。その理由の一つは、あんこ――日本ではおなじみの豆で作った甘いあん――と発音がまぎらわしいことである。

　ある外国人がまたスーパーマーケットを懸命に何度も歩き回っている。だが、探しているもの――あんこ――が見つからない。結局彼はひとりの店員の方に近づいて行った。

　「すみませんが」と、その外国人はたずねた。「ウンコはどこに置いてあるんでしょうか」。

　その女性店員はあっけにとられた様子だったが、「外国人ってアレをどこかに置くのかしら」と思いながら、トイレの方を指さしたという。

　神様の次に大切なものは海賊デス

Lowell doesn't get what's so funny. Yet he needs an answer.

"Where is **Unko**?"

Now the girls laugh so hard they have to claw at their throats to keep from gagging.

"No **Unko** here? Are you sure?"

Finally a girl in the front row raises her hand, with her ribs aching so painfully that her arm weighs a ton.

"So you're **Unko**!" Lowell beams.

"I thought it might be you! You have an **Unko** look."

This man later married a Japanese and you can well guess his wife's first name. Rumor has it he also screwed up his wedding vows.

"I take you **Unko**...to love, honor and comfort... "

THE various Japanese words for poop, manure and so on cause **gaijin** all sorts of problems, as we have previously seen with **koyashi**. **Unko** perhaps presents the greatest risk as it sounds razor close to **anko**, a term for sweet bean paste, *anko* a popular Japanese confection.

Again an earnest foreigner journeys round and round the supermarket to no avail. Finally he approaches a clerk.

"Excuse me," he says, "but where do you keep your poop?"

The woman is stunned, but then points towards the restroom, wondering, "Where do foreigners keep theirs?"

　　　　　　　　外国人は店で自分の欲しい品物が見つから
ないと、どこに置いてあるか店員によくたずねる。
　「すみませんが」と、ある男性がスーパーマーケットの店
員を呼びとめた。「シタギはどこに置いてありますか？」。
　シタギ（下着）とシイタケ（椎茸）は発音がよく似てい
るらしい。

　「すみませんが」と、あるガイジン男性がパン売場のカウ
ンターでたずねた。「キタナイパンはありますか？　わたし
はそういうパンが好きなんですけど」。キタナイ（汚い）は
キッテイナイ（切っていない）に似ている。
　「すみませんが」と、別の外国人が店の奥の鮮魚売り場
でたずねた。「イヌはありますか？」。
　「犬？」。店員は聞きちがえかと思った。
　「ええ」と、その客は続けた。「スシ屋で食べたんですけ
れど、気に入りました。自分で買ってみたいと思って」。
　「でも、日本人は犬なんか食べませんがねえ」と店員は
客に言った。
　それでも客はゆずらなかった。彼は自分は一度ならず
食べたことがあるし、おいしかったと言い張った。
　「どっちにしたって、うちには犬なんてありませんよ」。
　客はその場を離れたが、客も店員も少々腹をたててい
た。二人ともわかっていなかったのである。その外国人は
イヌとウニとをとりちがえていたのだ。イヌとウニはもち
ろんまったく違った動物なのだが、彼はuniという文字を
逆さにしてinuと思いこんでしまっていたのだった。

FOREIGNERS regularly ask for items that they can't find.

"Excuse me," a man stops a supermarket clerk. "Where do you keep your underwear?"

With the word for undies, **shitagi**, sounding appealingly close to **shiitake**, the word for mushrooms.

shitagi
shiitake

EXCUSE me," asks a man at the bread counter. "Do you have any dirty bread? I like it that way."

Kitanai being "dirty" and **Kitte inai** meaning "not sliced."

kitanai
kitte inai

"Excuse me," asks yet another foreigner back in the seafood section. "Do you have any dog?"

"Dog??" The clerk believes he has misheard.

"Yeah," the customer goes on. "I had some at a sushi shop and loved it. I want to buy some myself."

"But Japanese don't eat dog," the clerk tells him.

Yet, the customer is adamant. He has tried it more than once and insists it's delicious.

"In any case, we don't have any."

So the men part, both feeling a bit upset. And not understanding that the foreigner had come up with "dog"—**inu**—by reversing the letters in the word for a very different animal, **uni**...meaning "sea urchin."

inu
uni

「すみませんが」と、ある外国人女性があたりをはばかるように小声で言った。「ヒナンゼリーはありますか？」。彼女は薬局のカウンターの前に立っていた。

　「ヒナンゼリー？」。店員はびっくりした。そんなの一度も聞いたことがない。

　「ええ、ヒナンゼリーです。以前に何度も買ったことがあります」。

　「でも、それをどうなさるんですか？」。顔を赤らめている女性客に店員はたずねた。

　その客が本当に欲しかったのは、ヒナンゼリー——そんなものは存在しない——ではなく、ヒニンゼリー（避妊ゼリー）、すなわち殺精子剤だったのだ。

「すみませんが」と、別の外国人がたずねた。今度はコンビニのドリンクカウンターである。「苺のゴキブリはありますか？」。

　この外国人は、苺という言葉は正しく言うことができた。ところが、「かき氷」と言うべきところをまちがえて、「ゴキブリ」と言ってしまった。

　「苺はやってないんですよ。うちはチョコレートだけなんですよ」と、店員は答えたが、心の中ではたぶんあの例の色をしたゴキブリを思いうかべていたにちがいない。

神様の次に大切なものは海賊デス

EXCUSE me," hushes a foreign woman in a blooper courtesy of MANGAJIN magazine. "But do you have any disaster jelly?" She is standing in front of a pharmaceutical counter.

"Disaster jelly?" The clerk is dumbfounded. She has never heard of such a thing.

"Yes. Disaster jelly. I've bought it many times."

"But what do you do with it?" the clerk asks as the woman turns red.

For rather than non-existent "disaster jelly"—or **hinan zerî**—what she really wants is **hinin zerî**—a spermicide.

hinan zerî
hinin zerî

Which, depending on your view of kids, may indeed prevent disasters.

EXCUSE me," asks another foreigner, this one at the drink counter in a convenience store. "But do you have any **ichigo** roaches?"

While the man got **ichigo**, "strawberry," right, he booted the word for shaved ice... **kakigôri**. Instead he offered **gokiburi**, which means "cockroach."

kakigôri
gokiburi

"No. Here we just have chocolate," the attendant answers, envisioning perhaps roaches of the everyday color.

「すみませんが」と、病弱そうな外国人が恥ずかしそうに、日本語で口ごもりながら言った。ある家庭用電気器具の店で、彼は店員の方へちょうど近づいたところである。「わたしはソウシキが必要なのです。どこに行ったらいいでしょうか」。

　「この店以外ならどこへでもどうぞ」と、店員は思った。というか、彼の店はソウシキ（葬式）は取り扱わないが、ソウジキ（掃除機）なら売っている。

次の 言い間違いは店ではなく、郵便局で起こった。今度の外国人女性はなかなかの勉強家だった。日本に来てからまだ一年たらずだが、「もの」という接尾辞を動詞につけると、その動詞が名詞に変わるということを知っていた。たとえば、「食べる」という動詞の語尾に「もの」をつけると、「食べ物」という語になる。同様に、「飲む」という動詞にこの接尾辞をつけると、「飲み物」という名詞になる。この女性は今、エアメールに使う糊つきラベルが欲しかった。そして彼女は「付ける」という動詞を知っていた。

　「すみませんが」と、彼女は局員に言った。彼女の後ろには、手紙や箱を手にした人たちがずらりと長い列を作って並んでいた。「航空便用のツケモノはありますか？」。

　それは論理的な発想だった。だが、あいにくその言葉は漬物を意味したのである。

　一方では、別の外国人がスーパーマーケットの奥でまったく同じ言葉を言い間違えてしまった。この場合、彼女はまさに漬物を買おうとしたのだが。

　「すみませんが」と、彼女は言った。「スケベモノはありますか？」。これは正しい言葉ではないが、意味は明白で

神様の次に大切なものは海賊デス

EXCUSE me," hems a sickly looking foreign fellow in shy Japanese. He has just approached a clerk at an appliance store. "But I need a funeral. Where should I go?"

"Anyplace but here!" thinks the clerk.

Yet, while his shop may not provide **sôshiki** or "funerals," it does provide **sôjiki** or "vacuum cleaners." *sôshiki* *sôjiki*

THE next bloop happens not at a store, but at a post office. This time, the foreign woman is quite the student.

She's been in Japan less than a year and has learned that adding the suffix **mono** to verbs can change those verbs into nouns. For example, put **mono** on the end of **taberu**—to eat—and the result is the word for food—**tabemono**. Do the same thing with the verb **nomu**—to drink and you have **nomimono**—the noun form for "drink." In this case, the woman wanted airmail stickers and she knew the verb "to stick" was **tsukeru**.

"Excuse me," she asks the clerk. Behind her trails a long line of people holding letters and boxes. "But do you have any airmail **tsukemono**?" *tsukemono*

Logical. Unfortunately, **tsukemono** means pickles.

Meanwhile, another foreigner back at the supermarket glitches on the very same word, only this time she wants the pickles.

"Excuse me," she says. "Do you have any **sukebemono**?" *sukebemono*

ある。スケベ（助平）は好色を意味する。つまり、彼女は
店員にエロチックな品物が欲しいと言ったことになる。

「あー」。その男性店員は肩をすくめて言ったそうである。「バナナはいかがですか？」。

　　　　　　　　次の　外国人はまる
で違った苦況に陥った。彼の場
合、日本語がよくできて、敬語も
何とか使うことができた。彼をデ
ニスと呼ぶことにしよう。

　デニスは上司から署名をもらわ
なければならなかった。それも今
日中に必要だった。ところがその
日、上司はもうすでに退社してし
まっていた。

　めげずにデニスは上司の自宅ま
での行き方を書きとめて、急いで
会社を出た。上司の家には一時間もしないうちに到着し、
玄関のブザーを押した。

　「はい？」と、若い女性の声が聞こえた。

　デニスは自分の名前を告げて、会社からやって来たこ
とを説明した。玄関のドアが開けられた。

　Tシャツを着てジーンズをはいた女子高生が立ってい
た。なかなか魅力的な女子高生であった。とはいえ、さほ
どグラマーなタイプではなかった。

　デニスは言葉にまごついた。そのかわいらしい少女に
思わずみとれてしまった。彼女はそのやさしい無邪気な目

神様の次に大切なものは海賊デス

While not a true word, the meaning is clear enough, with **mono** meaning "thing" and **sukebe** meaning "lewd." In other words, she has asked the clerk for a lewd object.

"Uh..." the man is said to have shrugged. "How about bananas?"

THE next foreigner put himself in an entirely different pickle. In his case, his Japanese was competent enough to wrestle with honorific forms. Let's call him Dennis.

Dennis needed his boss's signature and he needed it before tomorrow. Yet, the boss had already left for the day.

Undaunted, Dennis scribbled down directions to the man's house and dashed off. He arrived in less than an hour and poked the doorbell.

"Yes?" came the voice of a young girl.

Dennis gave his name and explained he had come from the office. The door opened.

There stood an attractive high school girl in a T-shirt and jeans.

Yet, one not so very well endowed.

Dennis found himself searching for words. He couldn't help but gaze at the lovely girl, who blinked at him with

をぱちくりさせて、彼を見つめていた。

　「お父さんはどちらにいらっしゃいますか？」という意味のことをデニスは言うつもりだった。だが、デニスはそう言わなかった。彼は言った。「あなたのオチチはどこですか？」。

　「お」は丁寧を表す接頭語である。「ちち」は「父」を意味する語だが、デニスはまだそれが自分自身の親を指す場合のみに使われることを知らなかった。

　デニスはまた「おちち」が「乳房」を意味することも知らなかったのである。

　「あなたの乳房はどこですか？」とは、少女にとってはいささか答えに窮する質問であった。

別の 外国人はまったく異なる言葉を、まるきり正反対の状況で言い間違えた。

　今度の女性はグラマーなんて言葉では足りないぐらいだった。えりの大きくあいた袖なしを着たその女性は、いかにも男心をそそるようなタイプだった。

　実際のところ、その電車に乗りあわせた男性はみな彼女に視線を向けていた。その中のひとりがニックだった。彼女のとなりの席があいたとき、ニックはそのチャンスを逃さずとらえた。すかさずその機をとらえたとはいえ、彼は紳士としてのたしなみを忘れなかった。ニックはその若い女性の目の高さまで頭を下げた。二人のあいだには、一対のソフトボールのような彼女の乳房があった。彼女がニックの方に視線を向けたとき、彼はにやっと笑った。「座っていいですか？」と、ニックは言え

神様の次に大切なものは海賊デス

doe eyes.

"Uh, where is your father?" is what he meant to say.

But instead he blurted, "**Ochichi wa?**"   *ochichi*

With **O** being an honorific prefix and **chichi** being a   *chichi*
word for father, a word that Dennis had not yet learned
he should use only in reference to his own parent.

Neither had he learned that the word **ochichi** means
breasts.

With "Where are your breasts?" being a question the
girl did not quite know how to answer.

ANOTHER foreigner blooped with a completely different word in the exact opposite situation.

This time the girl was more than just endowed. In a
low cut, sleeveless top, she was downright enticing.

Indeed, every guy on the train had his eye on her—
including Nick. When the seat next to her opened, he
grabbed his chance.

But he did it with a gentleman's flare.

Nick lowered his head down to the girl's eye level—
her breasts hanging between them like a pair of soft-
balls—and when he had her attention, he grinned:

"May I sit?"

Only the verb "sit" starts with **su**—**suwaru**, with "May   *suwaru*
I sit?" being **Suwatte ii desu ka?** The verb Nick used was

ばよかったのだ。ところが実際には彼は「さわっていい
ですか？」と言った。その女性はだまって電車を降りた。

さあ、次はデビドの例である。彼の日本語はもう完璧
だった。ただ質問を間違えたにすぎない。

　まず知っていて欲しいのは、デイビッドが非常に探索好
きということだ。彼はたえずどこか有名な観光名所──とり
わけお決まりのコースから外れたへんぴな所にあるもの──
を探し出そうと懸命だった。

　その時は、山のふところ深くたたずむ名刹を探していた
ところだった。

　彼はある雑誌の記事を頼りにその寺へ行こうとしてい
た。しかし、目的地に近づいて、一車線の道路をぬうよう
に車を走らせ始めると、その記事が役にたたないことがわ
かってきた。愛車──日産車である──をあちこちに走ら
せたあげく、ついに明白な事実を認めざるを得なかった。
彼は道に迷ってしまったのである。

　だが、彼は前方にひとりの年配の日本人女性が小股で
歩いているのに気がついた。彼は彼女に道をたずねること
にした。

神様の次に大切なものは海賊デス

almost the same, only it began with **sa**—from the verb,
sawaru.   *sawaru*

And **Sawatte ii desu ka** means, "May I feel?" "May I
touch?" or "May I grope." The choice is yours.

As for the girl, she chose to get off.

NOW we come to David, whose language communicates
perfectly. He just asks the wrong question.

First understand David is the consummate explorer,
forever eager to sniff out some famous sight, especially
when off the beaten track.

This time he is on the search for a renowned temple, a
site enveloped deep in the hills.

He traces his way from descriptions in a magazine,
but once he draws near and begins weaving his way up
and down one-lane streets, the article proves useless.
Around and around he turns his Nissan, until he finally
has to admit the obvious. He is lost.

Yet, up ahead David spies an elderly Japanese woman,
mincing her way down the road. He decides to ask for
directions.

He rolls down his window and eases his Nissan to a
halt along side her. The woman leaps when she sees his

　彼は車の窓を下げた。それから車の速度をゆるめて、その女性のそばに止めた。ひげをたくわえた外国人の顔を見て、彼女はまるで森の中で獣にでくわしたかのようにとびあがった。

　「すみませんが」と、彼は日本語であいさつした。「ちょっと道に迷ってしまったんですが、おたずねしてもよろしいでしょうか？」。

　女性はほっとした。彼女はこれまでの長い人生で、生まれて初めてガイジンに出会ったのである。デビッドの話す日本語を聞いたとたん、見知らぬ外国人に対する彼女の警戒心は興味に変わっていった。

　不運なことに、そのときデビッドの日本語はたまたま言い間違いの世界に迷いこんでしまった。すなわち、彼は「お寺」と言うかわりに、「お手洗い」という言葉を選んでしまったのである。

　「わたしはオテアライを探しているのです」と、彼は彼女に言った。彼女はけげんな顔をした。「お手洗い？」。

　「ええ、このあたりに大きなオテアライがあるって雑誌で読んだんです」。

　女性は首をひねった。力になってあげたいとは思うのだけれど…。「申し訳ないんですけど、そんな場所は知りませんねえ」。

　がーん！　てことは、よっぽど深く迷ってしまったのか。

　「本当にご存じではないのですか」と、彼はたずねた。「そのオテアライは有名だと聞いています。毎日何百人もそこを訪れるという記事を読んだのですけれど」。

　女性はまた首を振った。「いいえ、このあたりには特別な場所ってないんですよねえ」。この言い方は、生理的要

神様の次に大切なものは海賊デス

bearded foreign face, as if coming head to head with a beast in the woods.

"Excuse me!" he greets in Japanese. "I'm a little lost. Could you help me?"

The woman relaxes. For the first in her long life she has met a gaijin and upon hearing David's Japanese, her mood swings from alarm to interest.

Unfortunately, David's Japanese then swings into Blooperland. Instead of the Japanese word for temple, **otera**, he chooses the word **otearai**.

otera

otearai

"I'm looking for a toilet," he tells her.

She wrenches her face. "A toilet?"

"Yeah, I read there's a big one near here."

"I'm sorry. I don't know of any such place."

Gosh, David worries, is he that lost?

"Are you sure?" he asks. "I've heard hundreds of people go there everyday."

Again she shakes her head. "Not around here. We have

求を感じたときには排出する場所を問わないという日本人
の一般的な考え方を認めているようにも聞こえる。

　「急いでらっしゃるの？ と申しますのも、わたしの家にもお
手洗いはありますから。ただ…そう大きくはありませんけれ
ど」。彼女はガイジンには大きなお手洗いが必要なのだろうと
考えていた。

　だが、デビッドは家庭にあるお寺、つまり仏壇には全然
興味がなかった。

　「いいえ、全然急いではいません。まだ二、三時間ありま
す。でも、とにかくありがとうございます」。彼はおじぎを
して礼を述べた。

　女性も彼におじぎをした。そして、その日産車は音をた
てて走り去った。

　「気の毒に」と、車が見えなくなると彼女は声に出して
言った。「何とか間に合うといいけど」。

　他方、デビッドはあきらめるどころではなかった。「た
とえ一日中かかっても、オテアライを見つけてやるぜ！」
と、彼は叫んだ。

　その一方、さしあたり今自分に必要なのはトイレであ
ることに、彼は気がついた。

神様の次に大切なものは海賊デス

no special spot at all." A nod perhaps to the general Japanese view that when nature calls any place will do.

"Are you in a hurry? 'Cause there's one at my house. But...it's not so big." And she supposes a gaijin does need a big one.

But David has no interest in a family altar. "No, no hurry at all. Thanks anyway." He bows his appreciation.

The woman bows back and the Nissan putters away.

Meanwhile, David has far from given up. "I'm gonna find that temple if it takes all day!" he yells.

On the other hand, what he could use right now, he realizes, is a toilet.

　　　　　　西洋人の目から見れば、日本人はトイレや肉体に関連したユーモアに対して比較的開放的な考えをもっている。このことを不快に思うガイジンもいれば、目新しくて面白いと思うガイジンもいる。

　レイは後者のグループに属する。彼は「お尻」という言葉を学んだ。また、この肉体の一部分に対する敬意を省略して言えば、「尻」と呼ぶことも知った。そして友人がトイレットペーパーをシリガミと呼ぶのを聞いた。

　レイの耳では「ちり」と「しり」の違いは聞き取れなかった。例の友人はちゃんとちり紙と言っているのだが、レイの耳にはシリガミと聞こえる。

　「ふーむ」と、レイは考えた。「これは面白い。日本人はトイレットペーパーを尻紙と呼んでいる。何てもっともなんだろう！」。

　予想外だったのは、レイの言い間違いは、だれかがそれを正すまで何年も続いたことである。

　振動がニトログリセリンの爆発を促すように、「お尻」という単語は外国人の言い間違いを誘う。日本語を学んでいる外国人にこの言葉を使わせてみるがいい。その結果たるやもう大変なものだ。たとえば、「お尻」はたえず「押入れ」と混同される。

　完璧なアパートを求めているスティーブは、いつも押入れが狭いことを不満に思っていた。さて、今彼はもうひとつの候補のアパートを見るために階段を登っていた。借りることになれば彼の新しい大家さんとなる女性が彼を案内していた。

　大家さんはスティーブを三つの部屋から成るアパート

神様の次に大切なものは海賊デス

IN Western eyes, Japanese have compara-
tively open ideas on toilet and body humor. This puts off
some gaijin, while others find it refreshing.

Ray fit this latter group. He learned the word for "butt"
was **oshiri**—or with not quite so much honor just **shiri**—
and then heard a friend refer to toilet paper as **chirigami**.

Now **chiri** and **shiri** are different words, with **chiri**
meaning "dust" or "rubbish." As **gami** or **kami** means
paper, **chirigami** refers to a rough-grained, cheaper form
of toilet paper, though most Japanese these days will simply say, **toiretto pepa**.

Yet, Ray's ears did not hear the difference. Instead, he
heard the man say **shirigami.**

"Hmm," thought Ray. "This is interesting. The Japanese call toilet paper, 'butt paper.' How natural!"

Predictably Ray then walked to the store and asked
for some butt paper. What is not so predictable is that he
did this for years till someone corrected his boo-boo.

shiri
chirigami
chiri

shirigami

THE word **oshiri** is to bloops what motion is to nitro.
Put a language learner and the word **oshiri** together and
just wait for the boom.

So there is no better word to lead us out of regular
questions and into the wider and wackier arena of
requests.

へ招じ入れた。彼は部屋を見回したが、清潔で日当たりがよかった。

「いい感じですね」と、彼は言った。女家主は顔をほころばせて彼を見た。彼も顔を輝かせて、彼女を見た。

「じゃあ、あなたのオシリを見せて下さい」彼は彼女に言った。「大きいといいなあ」。

スタン は別な体験をした。初めて訪れたとき、彼の新しいアパートは良い感じに見えた。ところが、二週間後そのアパートに引っ越してみて、すっかり汚れてるのにぎょっとした。とくに押入れはカビで縞模様ができていた。

彼は携帯電話のボタンを押した。「もしもし」と、彼は家主に言った。「僕のオシリはかびだらけなんです！僕はどうしたらいいですか？」。

家主はなんともアドバイスのしようがなかったようだ。

「では、僕のオシリをきれいにするのを手伝っていただけないでしょうか。かびだらけのオシリなんて、がまんできませんよ！」。

神様の次に大切なものは海賊デス

Where **oshiri** forever bumps with **oshi-ire**, the word *oshiri*
for closet.   *oshi-ire*

In his hunt for the perfect apartment, Steve has been
forever critical of limited closet space. Now he mounts
the stairs to see one further room candidate, with his potential new landlady leading the way.

The woman ushers Steve into the three-room flat,
where he spins around to find the place clean and sunny.

"Looks good," he says. The landlady then glows at
Steve, and Steve glows back.

"Now show me your butt," he tells her. "I hope it's a
big one."

STAN had a different experience. His new pad seemed
fine when he first visited, but when he moved in two
weeks later, he was appalled at all the dirt.

Particularly, he found his closet to be streaked with
mold.

He jabbed the buttons on his cell phone.

"Hey," he said to his landlord, "My butt is full of mold!
What do I do about that?"

The landlord, it seems, could offer no advice at all.

"Well, could you help me clean it? I can't live with a
moldy butt!"

さて、スージーと彼女の大家さんである山田さんとの関係はずっと良好だった。この老人は必ずしもスージーの外国式のやり方に賛成ではなかったが、彼女にぞっこん参っていた。彼女のためなら何事もいとわぬ思いだった。まあ..ほとんど何事も。

　ある朝山田さんの電話が鳴った。二階のスージーからだった。その前の一時間あまり階上で彼女が騒々しく動き回ったり、物を動かしたり、またトイレの水を流したりするのが聞こえた。

　「山田さんですか？」彼女が言った。「ちょっと困ったことがあるのです。助けていただけませんでしょうか？」

　かわいらしくて、きちんとした日本語だ。それを聞くと山田さんの顔がほころぶ。

　「いいですよ」と、彼は答えた。「どうしたのかな？」。

　「ええとですね」スージーは息を吸い込んだ。「大したことじゃないと思われるでしょうけれど...わたしのお尻がしまらないんです」。

　山田さんは受話器を取り落としそうになった。「何だって？」。

　「わたしのお尻がしまらないんです、昨夜からずっと。なぜこんな風になったのかわからないんですけど」。

　山田さんはスージーがトイレの水を流していた音を思い出した。「私にはわかっていたんだ」彼は考えた。「わたしはちゃんとわかっていたんだ、外国人に部屋を貸すべきではなかったということを」。

　「こんなことは以前にはなかったことです」スージーは言った。「詰まっているのかもしれません。でも、あたりをさわってみたんですが、何もありませんでした。といっても、ご存じでしょうが、ちょっと見えにくい場所ですから」。

神様の次に大切なものは海賊デス

NOW Suzy and her landlord, Mr. Yamada, had a much better relationship. Indeed the old man was smitten with Suzy—despite not always following her foreign ways. For Suzy there was nothing Mr. Yamada wouldn't do.

Well...almost nothing.

One morning, Mr. Yamada's phone rang. It was Suzy, calling from upstairs. For over an hour he had heard her banging around above him, moving things about and flushing the stool.

"Mr. Yamada?" she began. "I've got a small problem. Could you help me?"

Cute, precise Japanese that made Mr. Yamada smile.

"Certainly," he answered. "What is it?"

"Well," Suzy inhaled. "This may not sound like much but...my butt won't close."

Mr. Yamada almost dropped the phone. "What?"

"My butt won't close. Ever since last night. I don't know what's wrong."

Mr. Yamada remembered the sound of the flushing toilet. "I knew it," he thought. "I knew I shouldn't have rented to a foreigner."

　「そうだね」山田さんにもそれは理解できた。だがいったい、スージーはどのように助けて欲しいというのか？

　彼女は続けた。「二階に来て、手を貸していただければと思ったのですけれど。開けっぱなしになっている原因を見ていただけますか。もしくは、せめてこのしゃくにさわるオシリが何とか閉まるように手伝って下さい」。

　いまや山田さんは汗をかいていた。「医者にみてもらった方がいいとは思いませんか？」。

　電話の向うのスージーは黙ったままだった。山田さんは続けた。「あなたを病院へ車でつれていってあげてもいいんですよ。こちらは全然かまわないですから」。

　スージーが言った。「何だか誤解されているようですけれど。お昼を食べに友達が来ることになっているんです。それで、みんなが来る前にオシリをちゃんと閉めておきたいと思って。中に詰め込んだがらくたを友達に見られたくないんです」。

"This has never happened before," Suzy admitted. "I think it might be blocked, but I felt around and couldn't find anything. But, you know, it's kind of hard to see."

"Yes," Mr. Yamada could understand that. But what did Suzy want?

"I'm wondering," she continued. "If you could come up here and give me a hand. See if there's anything holding it open. Or at least help me squeeze the darn thing shut."

Now Mr. Yamada was sweating. "Don't you think, you could use a doctor instead?"

From Suzy's end came silence. Mr. Yamada went on. "I could drive you to a hospital. I don't mind."

She spoke: "I'm afraid you've lost me. But I'm having some company over for lunch and I want my butt closed before they arrive. I don't want them to see all the junk I've got jammed inside."

　　　　　　　「殺す」という日本語も伝説的な言い誤りを
生み出している。とりわけ、「殺して」という依頼の形で
の言い間違いが顕著である。というのも、「おろして」と
よく混同されるからである。

　今日アレックスはバスのずっと奥へ押しやられてしまっ
た。早朝のラッシュ時は、みんなが頭を下に向けているも
のだから、彼と出口の間には黒い髪の海が広がっている。

　バスは他の車の間をじりじり進んで行く。車内のアレック
スは何とか前に出ようとするのだが、他の乗客はあまり道を
あけてはくれない。その上に、停留所にとまるたびにさらに
大勢が乗り込んでくる。

　自分が降りる停留所に近づいてバスが速度を落とし始める
と、アレックスはよろよろと前方へ向かった。だが、前に進
むことができない。あわてふためいて、彼は大声を出した。
彼は今までに日本人がそうするのをよく見かけていた。ただ
彼の場合は言うべき言葉を間違えた。

　「わたしをコロシテ下さい！」彼は叫んだ。「お願いだか
ら、わたしをコロシテ下さい！ わたしを今コロシテくだ
さい！」。

　すぐにみなが目をさました。それだけではなく、彼らは
アレックスがバスを降りるまで敬遠して、そばに寄ろうと
しなかった。

ミッチェル のやり方はもう少し洗練されていた。停留所の
名前を聞き取る自信がない上に、バスの道順を知らなかっ
たので、彼は運転手の近くに場所を陣取った。

　「お願いです」と、彼は運転手に言った。「郵便局に着い
たら、どうぞわたしをコロシテ下さい。いいですね？」。

神様の次に大切なものは海賊デス

THE Japanese word **korosu**, meaning "to kill," has also led to some legendary bloopers. Especially in request form—**koroshite**. For it is often confused with the verb **orosu**, with **Oroshite kudasai** meaning "Please let me off."

koroshite

oroshite

Today Alex found himself pretzelled far into the back of the bus, a sea of dark hair between him and the exit, everyone with their heads bowed in the early morning rush.

With the bus edging through traffic, Alex tried to worm his way forward, but the crowd didn't give much and at each new stop even more people ploughed on.

So now as the bus slowed for his stop, Alex lurched forward...with no headway. Panicking, he spoke up, as he had often seen Japanese do. He just picked the wrong word.

"Kill me!" he cried. "Please kill me! Kill me now!"

At once everyone woke up. And not only that, they gave Alex an extra wide berth till he was off the bus.

MITCHELL'S method was a bit more refined. Uncertain of his ability to hear the stops and not knowing the route of the bus, he secured a spot close to the driver.

"Listen," he told the man. "When we get to the post office, please kill me. OK?"

　「おかす」という動詞にまつわる言い間違いも伝説的といっていい。この言葉は不当にも「おこす」に似ている。この二語の依頼の形はそれぞれ「おかして」、「おこして」となる。実際のところ、人に犯して欲しいと頼む者はあまりいない。だが、次の話に登場する二人の外国人女性は別である。

　最初の話の舞台はあるホテルである。若い外国人女性が、クラークが後ろで立って用紙に押印している間、辛抱強く机に向かって待っていた。ついにクラークが彼女に気づいた。

　「何かご用でしょうか？」と、彼は聞いた。

　女性は必殺の笑顔を見せた。クラークがかわいかったから。「ええ」と、彼女はいたずらっぽくウインクして彼に言った。「どうぞわたしを6時に犯して下さいね」。

　次も 同じ動詞をめぐる話で、状況だけでなく頼んでいる時刻さえも同じである。ただ、話の舞台だけが違う。

　ダイアンはハイスクールの交換学生で、ホームステイ先の父親の方へ近づいて言った。「お願いしたいことがあるんですが、いいですか？」。

　父親は新聞をおいて、眼鏡を押し上げた。「もちろん」と、彼は答えた。

　「明日の6時に私を犯してくれませんか。そうしてもらうと、とてもありがたいのですけれど」。

　男は犯してくれなどとはまず頼まないが、次の男性は頼んだに近い。彼はデパートの紳士服売り場の女店員に近づいて大声で叫んだ。「ワイセツお願いします！」。

神様の次に大切なものは海賊デス

Yet another verb of mythical blooper stature is **okasu**, *okasu* which is unfairly similar to **okosu**. Now **okosu** means *okosu* "to wake" with the request form of **okoshite** registering as "Wake me." **Okasu**, on the other hand, means "to rape." In truth, not many people ever make the request of **okashite**—"Rape me"—perhaps, in fact, only the two foreign women in the stories below.

The first takes place at a hotel. The foreign girl waits patiently at the desk, while the clerk behind stands stamping forms. At last, he notices.

"Can I help you?" he asks.

The girl flashes a knockout smile. For the clerk is cute.

"Yeah," she tells him with a flirty wink. "Please rape me at six."

NEXT, same verb, same situation, even same time. Just a different place.

Diane, a high school exchange student, approaches her homestay father. "Can I ask you a favor?" she begs.

The father sets down his paper and pushes up his spectacles. "Sure," he answers.

"Could you rape me tomorrow at six? I'd really appreciate it."

Men do not often ask to be raped, but the following guy came close. He marched up to a female clerk on the men's floor of a department store and sharply cried:

"**Waisetsu onegai shimasu!**" *waisetsu*

Which means, "I'd like to be molested." **Waishatsu**, *waishatsu* on the other hand, means "a men's business shirt."

別の外国人女性はもっと微妙な迫り方をしたようだ。「わたしにホテルを見せてちょうだい」日本人男性とのデートの際に、彼女は彼にささやいた。彼はじきに衿をゆるめ、息をした。彼は以前からアメリカの女性たちは、日本の女性たちとちがって、こういうことに関しては、進んでいると聞いていた。

　ところが、彼はとんだ間抜け役を演じてしまった。というのは、ラブホテルに車をとめたときにわかったのだが、彼女の方では「ホテル」ではなく「ホタル」と言ったつもりなのである。蛍は日本のいたる所で観光の目玉となっている。駐車場には蛍は一匹もいなかったが、青年の顔は赤くなった。

　しかしながら、そんな言い間違いも次に紹介する宣教師の言い間違いに比べれば大したことではない。

神様の次に大切なものは海賊デス

ANOTHER foreign girl seemed to take a more subtle approach. "Show me a hotel," she cooed to her Japanese date—who immediately loosened his collar for breath. Yet he had long heard American girls were forward in such matters, unlike those back home.

But the joke was on him. For when he pulled up at the love hotel, he found the girl had not meant hotel—**hoteru** in Japanese—but **hotaru**, with the latter being a firefly, a sightseeing highlight throughout Japan.

hoteru

hotaru

While there were no fireflies in the parking lot, the boy's face lit up like one.

Japanese Made Funny

その宣教師はどちらかと言えばまだ若い男だったが、ある大学——女子大である——の門の外に立ってビラを配っていた。それは学生たちに自分の聖書の授業に参加を呼びかけるビラだった。女子大生ひとりひとりに彼は言った。「おヨメになって下さい！」。

彼としては「お読みになって下さい」と言っているつもりだった。

まあしかし、似たようなこととも言える。ある意味では。

というのも、彼はちゃんと「になって下さい」というかなり丁寧な依頼の表現を用いている。あいにくなのは、「読む」の丁寧な形は「お読み」である。「おヨメ」では花嫁の意味になってしまう。

「おヨメになって下さい」は「わたしの花嫁になって下さい」と言っているのと同じである。

その場で返事をしてくれる女子大生はひとりもいなかったが、彼の次の聖書の授業は超満員だった。

別の宣教師の場合である。日曜日の集会は賛美歌で始まった。それがすむと、彼は会衆に「チャクリクして下さい」と言った。

「着席」を「着陸」と言い間違えたのだ、まるでその教区民たちには天使のように翼があるみたいに。

本章最後の言い間違いにまつわる話にも天使が登場するが、この天使はもっとずっと世俗的な天使である。

神様の次に大切なものは海賊デス

NONE of the above bumblers, however, blooped to the extent of the following missionary.

In an effort to attract college kids to his Bible class, the missionary, a rather young fellow, stood outside a university gate—in this case at an all girls' school—handing out flyers.

To each girl he begged, "**Oyome ni natte kudasai!**"

Which he thought meant, "Please read this!"

And he was close. Sort of.

For **ni natte kudasai** is a very polite request form. Unfortunately, the corresponding polite form of "to read" is **oyoMI**. While **oyoME** means..."bride." *oyomi*

With **Oyome ni natte kudasai** equating to "Please be *oyome* my bride!"

While no one gave him an answer right away, his next Bible class overflowed.

ANOTHER missionary, after the opening Sunday hymn, told his congregation to **chaku riku shite kudasai**.

Now **chaku seki** is "sit down," while **chaku riku** *chaku seki* means "come in for a landing." As if the parishioners had *chaku riku* wings, like angels.

　　　　　　　　　この 話に関連して、「すわる」と「さわる」
を再びみてみよう。「すわる」という動詞の意味するとこ
ろは悪気がない。それに対して、「さわる」はこれから紹
介する男性たちにとって、願ってもないような意味合いを
もつ。

　ホスピタリティ・ディレクター（接待担当役員）として
のキャシーの任務のひとつは、公務でその会社を訪れたひ
とびとがオフィスや工場を見学するのを案内することであ
る。日本から訪問客がやって来ることもよくある。そこで
キャシーはわざわざ時間をとって基本的な日本語の表現を
頭に詰め込んだ。

　今日キャシーは日本人技師のグループを来客室のひと
つに待たせてある。遅刻気味だったので、彼女は同僚たち
ににこやかにあいさつしながら廊下を足早に歩いていく。
彼女は長身で、ブロンド。ヒップは見事な曲線を描き、肉
付きもいい。実際のところ彼女のブラウスの胸元はもうは
ちきれんばかりで、その胸元の一部が実にソソる感じで
ちょっとだけ見えている。ふたつのしっかりとした丘の斜
面は見惚れるような谷間で隔てられている。

　キャシーは来客室に到着すると、急いで中に入った。

　礼儀正しいその日本人客たちは、ドアが開くとすぐに
さっと立ち上がった。背広を着た三人の中年男性がいる
と、ただでさえ狭い部屋がさらに狭く見える。

　キャシーは男たちがいきなり立ち上がったのにびっく
りした。男たちの方でも同様に、この美人のほとんど神秘
的ともいえる容姿に驚きを感じた。腕を伸ばせば楽々と届
く近さに彼女は立っている。こんな女性が入ってくるとは
思ってもいなかった。

神様の次に大切なものは海賊デス

OUR final blooper in this chapter involves an angel of a more earthly type.

For this request, we return to **suwaru** and **sawaru**. **Suwaru** being the harmless verb "to sit" and **sawaru** being, in the case of the men below, the verb of their dreams, the verb "to feel."

suwaru
sawaru

One of Cathy's jobs as Hospitality Director is to conduct tours of the company office and plant for official guests. As these guests include frequent visitors from Japan, Cathy has put in extra hours boning up on fundamental Japanese.

Today she has a group of Japanese engineers waiting for her in one of the guest rooms. A bit late, she walks briskly down the hall, smiling "hellos" to coworkers. Cathy is tall. She is blond. She is curvy-hipped and buxom.

In fact, her blouse is stretched to the limits by her breasts, the upper slopes of which peek out in a tasteful manner, two firm hillsides separated by an enchanting valley.

She reaches the guest room and rushes inside.

Eager to be polite, the Japanese visitors spring to their feet as soon as the door is opened. Three middle-aged men in business suits, they make the tiny room seem even tinier.

Cathy is startled by their sudden standing. The men are equally startled by the almost magical appearance of this beautiful woman, less than an arm's length away.

　一瞬キャシーと男たちは驚いた表情で互いに見合った。男たちの目はいやおうなしに彼女の豊かな胸にひきつけられる。彼女の方が彼らよりも背が高い。彼女の胸はちょうど彼らの目の高さに突き出ている。

　キャシーの方が先に我に返って、魅惑的な微笑みをすぐに浮かべた。両腕を大きく広げて身振りをする。すると、彼女の胸の谷間がさらに前に突き出てくる。

　「どうぞ」と彼女は彼らに日本語で言う。「そんなに改まる必要はありませんわ。さあどうぞ、さわって下さい」。

　たぶん男たちは考えたに違いない。「なるほど、これがホスピタリティというものか」。

神様の次に大切なものは海賊デス

She is not what they had expected.

For a heartbeat Cathy and the men exchange astonished looks—with the eyes of the men irresistibly drawn to her ripe breasts. For she is taller than the guests and her bosom pokes forward right at eye level.

Cathy recovers first and breaks into an alluring smile. She gestures wide with her arms—serving to thrust her cleavage forward.

"Please," she tells them in Japanese. "There is no need to be so formal. Go ahead and feel."

With the men perhaps thinking... "Now this is hospitality."

海は空揚げでいっぱいです

観察や告白の言い間違い

██████████外国人 の目は日本人が見逃している多くのも
のをとらえている。

日本人が物事をただあるがままに見ているとき、外国人は
同じ物事をまるで思いもかけない風に見ている。というか、
少なくとも彼らの話を聞いていると、思いもかけない風に見
ているとしか思えないことがある。未熟な語学力という歪ん
だレンズを通して物事を見るとき、外国人はしばしば驚くべ
きことを発見するものである。このような「発見」の大部分
は、その生まれ故郷である言い間違いの海へ投げ返してあげ
るべきなのだろう。しかしながら、投げ返してしまうにはい
ささか惜しい「発見」もある。

神様の次に大切なものは海賊デス

THE WATER'S FULL OF FRIED CHICKEN

*Observations and confessions
of Japan's foreign guests*

FOREIGN eyes catch a lot that Japanese eyes don't.

For while Japanese simply see things as they are, foreigners will see the same things as they were never meant to be.

Or at least it can sound like they do. For life viewed through the warped lens of imperfect language can lead to some amazing discoveries.

Perhaps most of these "catches" should get tossed right back into the bloopery seas from which they came.

Yet, here are a few of the keepers...

「きみたーち、海に入っちゃダメだよー！」
ある外国人男性が、小学生の女の子たちのグループが海岸
に打ち寄せる波の中に足を踏み入れようとしているのを止
めさせようとして言った。

「そのへんにはクラゲがいっぱいいるよー！」。

彼はそう言いたかったのだ。でも、この男性は「クラゲ」
とは言わずに「からあげ」ということばを使ってしまっ
た。その結果は...

「きみたーち、海に入っちゃダメだよー！　そのへんには
空揚げがいっぱいいるよー」。

たしかに、揚げ物は体に良くないと医者はよく言うが。

さて、季節は秋へと移っていく。上と同じ外国人男性が散
りもみじを踏みしめながら、森の中の道を歩いて行く。

「きみたーち！」その男性はまたまた大慌てで手を振っ
ている。今度の相手はハイキング中の女子高生ふたり。
「そっちの方へ行ってはダメだよー。僕はそのへんで大き
なエビを見たよー！」。

本当は、彼は「エビ」ではなく「ヘビ」と言ったつもり
だった。

「冗談で言ってるんじゃないぞ！」彼は両手を拡げてそ
の大きさを示した。「こーんなに大きかったんだぞー！」。

エビ(shrimp)は英語では小エビを意味する。したがって
「大きいshrimp」は「短い長電話」と同じ矛盾語法である。
森の中に大きなエビがいても必ずしも矛盾とは言えまい
が、少なくとも不気味ではある。そのことに、男は全く気
付かなかった。

神様の次に大切なものは海賊デス

GIRLS, girls! Don't go in the water!" A foreign man tries to stop a group of grade-schoolers from wading out into the surf. "It's full of jellyfish!!"

Well...that's what he wished to say, with the word for jellyfish being, **kurage**. Instead the man has used **karaage**, which results in...

kurage
karaage

"Girls, girls! Don't go in the water! It's full of fried chicken!"

Of course, doctors do say fried foods aren't good for you.

NOW we move ahead to the fall, where we find the very same man tramping through a forest of autumn leaves.

"Girls, girls!" Again the man waves frantically, this time at a pair of high school hikers. "Don't go that way! I saw a big snake there!"

Only rather than snake—**hebi**—the man has said **ebi**, "shrimp."

hebi, ebi

"No kidding, girls!" The man stretches out his arms to show the size. "It was this long!"

With a "big shrimp" qualifying as an oxymoron. Our man, meanwhile, qualifies as another sort of moron.

「さあ、ここです！」ドイツ訪問中の日本人観光客を相手に、日本語のできるドイツ人バスガイドが言った。「窓の外をよーく見ていて下さい。この森の中では、かわいらしいウナギが道端の草をかじっている姿がよく見られるんですよ！」。

すぐに日本人乗客たちはバスの窓の方を向いた。森の中にウナギ！？　草をかじるかわいらしいウナギ！？　日本では到底見れそうもないそんな光景をぜひこの目で見たいと思って胸をワクワクさせながら。だが、期待は裏切られた。というのも、このガイドの言う「ウナギ」は、実は「ウサギ」のことだったからだ。まあ、ウサギだって見る価値は十分あるわけだが…。

　　　　　　日本語ではふつう英語の「cute」を「かわいい」と表わす。そして「frightening(恐ろしい)」を「こわい」と表わす。これほど意味の違うふたつの言葉がこれほど発音が似ているとは、なんと残酷な話ではあるまいか。
　　　　ある外国人女性が、近所の人の生まれたばかりの赤ちゃんの上にかがみこみ、かん高い声をあげた。「まあ〜、なんて恐いんでしょう！」。

日本語の「バス」は英語の「bus」の意味。一方、「ブス」はかなり不器量な女性をさす。この二つの言葉の類似はより一層残酷と言えるのではないだろうか。

神様の次に大切なものは海賊デス

"**AND** now!" says the German tour guide in this classic blooper from *Mangajin* magazine. "Keep your eyes fixed along the shoulder. For here in the forest we often spy cute rabbits nibbling on the roadside grass."

At once the Japanese passengers all press themselves to the bus window, anxious to see a sight they had heretofore thought impossible.

For the guide had blipped with rabbit—**usagi**—and instead presented the term **unagi**.

usagi
unagi

Most passengers not knowing "eels" lived in the forest. Or ate grass. Or might be considered cute.

THE Japanese word for cute is **kawaii**. The word for frightening is **kowai**. Cruel, isn't it, how close they are?

kawaii
kowai

A foreign woman bends over her neighbor's newborn baby. "Oh how frightening!" she squeals.

THE Japanese word for "bus" is a borrowed term from English—**basu**. The word for a remarkably ugly girl is **busu**. Keeps getting crueler, doesn't it?

basu
busu

　「ご存じかも知れませんが」と、バス停に立っていた外国人男性が隣の日本人に言った。「私の母国ではブスが来るまで相当待たされます。ところがここ東京ではブスは数分おきにやって来ますね。それも実に規則正しく」。

　その隣人が男性であったことを祈ろう。

日本語 の「血」と「火」もまぎらわしい。

　「ドクター、私を助けて下さい！」その電話をかけてきた外国人はパニック状態だった。「どうしたらいいかわかりません！ 私は火を吐いてしまったんです！」。

　医学的奇跡を実現したこの外国人は、幸いなことに生き延びて、次のような電話を水道業者にかけている。ここで奇跡をもたらしたのは「燃えている」と「漏れている」という二つの言葉であった。再びこの外国人はあわてふためいて叫んだ...

　「お願いです、私を助けて下さい！うちの風呂で水が燃えています！」。

神様の次に大切なものは海賊デス

"You know," says the foreign man, standing by the bus stop. "Back home we have to wait and wait for an ugly girl to pass on by. But here in Tokyo one comes along every few minutes. Just like clockwork."

THE word for "blood" is **chi**. The word for "fire," **hi**. *chi, hi*

"Doctor, you gotta help me!" The foreigner on the phone is in a panic. "I don't know what to do! I just coughed up some fire!"

Fortunately this medical marvel lived long enough to make the following phone call to his plumber. In this case, the mischievous word pair is **moete iru** and **morete** *moete iru*
iru, two verb construc- *morete iru*
tions that mean "burning" and "leaking," respectively. Yep, once more the foreigner panicked and yelped...

"Listen! You gotta help me! My bathtub's burning!"

　　　　　　　　さて、　今度は外国からやって来た交換留学
生の話。彼女は「優しい」と「野菜」を取りちがえた。そ
うとは気付かぬまま、あるとき彼女は日本人に陽気に感謝
の言葉を述べた。

　「この学校の先生はみんな野菜でーす。生徒も野菜でー
す。このことを私はとても喜んでいまーす。それは、わた
しがしょっちゅうドジ(dip)ばかりしてるからでーす」。

　この最後の一行はなんとなく「つくり」のにおいがす
る。というのも、英語のdipには「ドジ」と「野菜のつけ
汁」の両方の意味があるからだ。

次の　男は口を閉じたままでいればよかったのにと悔やん
でいる。

　「気がついた?」とガイジン社員が日本人の同僚に言っ
た。「このビルのトイレはみんなひどい味がするよ」。彼は
「味」と「臭い」を取りちがえたのだった。

「気が　ついた?」と別のガイジンが別の同僚に言った。「こ
のビルのどこにもまともな売春ってないんじゃない?」。
そんなものがあるべきだろうか?　間違えてはいけない。
あるべきなのは、まともな「売店」である。

神様の次に大切なものは海賊デス

NOW we have a foreign exchange student switching the words **yasashii** and **yasai**. **Yasashii**, in this case, means "gentle" or "kind." But if you use the other word it comes out as:

yasashii
yasai

"All the teachers in this school are vegetables! The students too! This pleases me so much—as most of the time I'm such a dip."

Well, perhaps she didn't add that last line.

OUR next guy, however, wishes he'd kept his mouth shut altogether.

"Have you ever noticed," says a gaijin office worker to his Japanese buddy, "that all the toilets in this building taste lousy?"

Mixing up the sense of taste—**aji**—with that for smell, **nioi**.

aji
nioi

"HAVE you ever noticed," says another gaijin to another buddy, in a blooper borrowed from *Mangajin* magazine, "that there's no decent prostitution in our whole building?"

With **baishun** being "prostitution" and **baiten** being "snack counter. "

baishun
baiten

「気が ついた？」と、さらにまた別の外国人サラリーマンが言った。「うちのトンカツ部長は太ってきたね」。

　これは、もし彼の勤務先が外食産業に分類される会社なら、場合によってはさほどおかしくは聞こえないかもしれない。しかし実際には、彼の勤務先は銀行だった。体重の増加を指摘されたのは、統括部長だったのである。

この 銀行員はおそらく次の発言をした人と同一人物であろう。「日本の金魚は引き続きもがき苦しむだろう。彼らは生き残れるのだろうか」。

　実のところ、日本の金魚には特に問題はないようである。問題があるとすれば、日本の企業であろう。

　　　　　　　日本 の女性については、外国人男性はたいてい彼女たちを非常によく観察している。というよりたぶん、観察し過ぎていると言えるだろう。次の二つの言い間違いの例で見てみると...

博多 は福岡県の一都市だが、博多美人と言えば、福岡県出身の美しい女性全体を意味することも多い。ここに登場する外国人男性は、日本人の同僚の妻が福岡出身ということを知っていた。彼はその女性に偶然出会った。そのとき彼女はひとりで、夫は一緒ではなかった。後で外国人男性は職場でその同僚をひじで突いて言った。

　「やあ、今日、きみの奥さんに会ったよ。奥さんはまさに博多美人だね」と、彼は言おうとしたのだ。しかし、美

神様の次に大切なものは海賊デス

"HAVE you ever noticed," says one further foreign office worker, "That our Fried Pork Manager is gaining weight?"

Not so funny perhaps, until you realize this is a bank. **Tokatsu**, or "overall," has fallen victim to **tonkatsu**, "fried pork."

tokatsu
tonkatsu

THIS office worker above is perhaps the same one who also observed: "Japanese goldfish continue to flounder. Can they survive?"

Yet Japanese goldfish—or **kingyo**—seem to be healthy. The same, however, cannot always be said for Japanese **kigyô**—or companies.

kingyo

kigyô

TURNING to Japanese girls, most foreign men can be very observant, perhaps even too observant. As in the next two bloopers...

FIRST understand that **Hakata** is a another name for Fukuoka and **bijin** means "beautiful woman." **Hakata bijin** thus refers to a beautiful woman from Fukuoka.

Hakata
bijin

In this case, again spun from *Mangajin*, our foreigner knows the wife of his Japanese colleague hails from Fukuoka. He runs into the woman separate from her husband and then later elbows the man back at work.

"Hey, I saw your wife today. And she's a real **Hakata Bijin**!"

人という言葉はちゃんと言うことができたのだが、「博多」を「はだか」と言ってしまった。したがって同僚が聞かされた言葉は...

　「やあ、今日、きみの奥さんに会ったよ。奥さんはまさに、裸美人だね！」。

　夫君はさぞかし驚いたことだろう。

　「おや」と、別の外国人男性が言った。彼はすらりとした脚の若い女性がかかとの高い靴をはいているのを見て驚き、彼女をじろじろ見た。そして声をかけた。その超ミニ姿の女性は通りを闊歩していたが、つかつかとその男の方へ歩み寄り、平手でぴしゃりと打った。男は「靴が高いね」と言うつもりで、「ケツが高いね」と言ってしまったからだった。

　このぴしゃりと打たれた男は、他人はいつもツイているのに自分ときたら常に不運に見舞われていると、ひがんでいるかもしれない。もしそうだとしたら、次の諺にもあるガイジンの知恵を処方箋とするのがいいかもしれない。その諺とは「他人のクソは青く見える」である。それは「他人の草」の間違いではないか、と人は思うかも

神様の次に大切なものは海賊デス

Which is what he tried to say. While he got the **bijin**
right, the foreigner replaced **Hakata** with the word   *hadaka*
hadaka. Which resulted in the
startled husband hearing:

"Hey, I saw your wife today.
And she's a real nude beauty!"

"MY!" says another foreign visitor, this one as presented
on *Karakuri Funniest TV* on TBS. "What tall shoes you
have!" The man is perusing a slim-legged girl parading
down the street in a short-short miniskirt—a girl who
steps right up to the guy and slaps him.

For instead of saying "**Kutsu ga takai ne**!" as he in-   *kutsu*
tended—with **kutsu** being "shoes" and **takai** being "tall,"
he has told her, "**Ketsu ga takai ne**!"   *ketsu*

Meaning, "My! Your rump is high!"

PERHAPS this battered fellow is one who
feels forever a victim of rotten luck, with other people
always getting the breaks. If so, he may then prescribe to
the following bit of proverbial **gaijin** wisdom.

"The other man's **kuso** is always greener."

Now **kusa** with a final "a" means "grass." **Kuso**, per   *kuso*

知れない。その通り。しかしこの言い間違いによる間違った人生観は私たちを観察から告白へと導いてくれる。というのも、日本に住む外国人たちはしょっちゅう自分たち自身について、また自分たちの生き方について、驚くような、人に言わずには済ませられないような新発見をしているからなのである。

　まずここに紹介するのは、例の紛らわしい「くさ」の語尾の言い誤りのもうひとつのケースである。このしくじりのせいでその男性はすっかり迷路にはまってしまった。ここで打ち明け話をしている紳士をジャックと呼ぶことにしよう。

　ある日昼食をとりながらジャックの日本人の同僚がたずねた。「あなたの故国での生活で懐かしく思うのはどんなことです？」。

　ジャックは考えた。戸外の陽気はすばらしかった。春の陽射しもまばゆく、頬を撫でるようなそよ風、そして新芽を出しかけた木々。

　「ものすごくというわけじゃないけれど」と、ジャックは告白した。「ちょっと懐かしいと思うことがひとつあるんです。あるいは馬鹿馬鹿しい事と思われるかもしれませんが」。

　その同僚は身をのりだした。「馬鹿馬鹿しい」という言

神様の次に大切なものは海賊デス

above, has the meaning per below:

"The other man's poop is always greener."

For **kuso** is another of those pesky words for excrement.

This bit of philosophy thus helps us swing from observations into confessions. For guests in Japan are continually making startling revelations about both themselves and the way they live.

For starters here is another case where the same wayward ending for "grass" led the man who misused it straight into Blooperland. Let's call this confessing gentleman Jack.

One day over lunch, Jack's Japanese coworker asks, "What's something you miss about life back home?"

Jack thinks. Outside the weather is gorgeous—a sparkling spring day with a teasing breeze and budding trees.

"I don't miss that much," Jack admits, "But there is one small thing that you'll probably think to be silly."

His lunchmate leans forward, the word "silly" alerting him to expect the unusual.

"Here in Japan, no one ever walks outside without shoes. Well, that's what I miss, especially on a day like today. For what I really like is to yank off my shoes and socks, leap out the door and..."

And here is where Jack bloops. For instead of saying **kusa**, like he intends, he says you know what.

"...walk atop some poop."

His lunchmate at once leans back. "Excuse me?" he asks.

葉が何か普通でないことを期待させたのだ。

「日本では、だれも靴をはかずに外を出歩こうとはしないですよね。これが私にはさびしく思われんです、とりわけ今日のような日にはね。私が本当に好きなのは靴も靴下もさっと脱いで、外にとびだす。そして、...」。

ここでジャックはしくじった。「草」のつもりで、彼が言ってしまったのは...

「... クソの上を歩くことなんです」。

相手はすぐに身を引いた。そして「なんとおっしゃいました？」と聞いた。

しかし、ジャックは今うっとりとした様子で目を閉じている。

「クソはとても気持ちいいんですよ！新しいのは特にね！私は足の指でクソをできるだけ強く踏みつけるのが好きでしてね。そしてゆっくりと歩き回る。それはもう天国ですよ」。

ジャックは目を開けた... 相手は彼の方をじっと見つめている。

「とにかく、これができないのが残念ですね。裸足でクソの上を歩き回れないのが」。

ジャックの真向いに座っていた相手はのどをごくりとさせて言った。「でも、それって汚くありませんか？」。

「少しはね」と言って、ジャックはうなずいた。「だけど、もし気持ちよければ... 私は「やっちゃえ！」と言いたいですね」。

But now Jack closes his eyes in ecstasy.

"It feels so fantastic! Especially when it's fresh! I just like to scrunch my toes down as tight as I can. And then prance slowly about. It's heavenly."

Jack opens his eyes...to find his friend staring at him.

"Anyhow, that's what I miss. Walking around barefoot on poop."

The man across from him swallows. "But isn't that dirty?"

"A little," Jack nods. "But if it feels good...I say 'Do it!' "

　　　　　　　さて、キムもジャックと同じ質問を向けられ
たが、彼女の答え方はまるで異なっていた。彼女の場合、
その会話は美容院でなされた。そして、彼女が懐かしがっ
ているのは「クソ」ではなく家族だった。だから、キムは
家族が懐かしいと言った。というか、少なくとも言ったつ
もりだったのだが...

　キムの髪型の仕上げに最後のはさみを入れながら、美
容師は雑談を始めた。「あなたの母国での生活で、懐かし
いと思われるのは何ですか？」と、美容師はたずねた。

　キムはすぐに答えた。「ああ、それは海賊です！海賊が
とても懐かしいです！」。

　美容師はカットの手を止めた。「アメリカに、海賊が、
いらっしゃるんですか？」。

　「ええ、大勢いますよ。ほとんどはテキサスにですが、
オクラホマにも何人かいます」。

　「それで...そういう人たちがいないのが寂しいんです
か？」。

　「ええ、もちろん寂しいです。海賊はいつだって大歓迎
してくれます。みんなが私を抱きしめたり、キスしてくれ
ます。それにすごいご馳走を出してくれます。彼らに会う
のはとっても楽しいです」。

　美容師はその外国人の顔をじっと見た。キムは目を閉
じて座っている。

　「あなたもご存じでしょうけれど、海賊は決して裏切ら
ないものです。他人は裏切ることがあるかもしれないけれ
ど、海賊は大丈夫。最後まで味方です」。

　そう言って、キムはおもむろに目をあけた。美容師は驚き
でまゆをしかめ、その表情は疑問でいっぱいのようだった。

神様の次に大切なものは海賊デス

NOW Kim received the very same poser, but responded in a very different way. In Kim's case, the conversation took place in a beauty shop. And it wasn't "poop" that Kim missed, but rather "family"—which in Japanese is **kazoku**.

kazoku

Yet, Kim said she missed **kaizoku**, with an extra **i** in-side. In fact, she claimed to miss **kaizoku** dearly. As you can see below:

kaizoku

The beautician made small talk as she snipped the last touches into Kim's hairdo. "What's something you miss about life back home?" she sought.

Kim's immediate an-swer:

"Oh, pirates! I miss them so much!"

The woman stopped in mid-snip "You have pirates in America!?"

"Uh huh. Many. Mostly in Texas, but some up in Oklahoma, too."

"And...you miss these people?"

"Oh, of course. They always throw such big welcomes. Hugs, kisses and huge meals. It's so nice to see them."

The beautician studied the foreign face. Kim sat with her eyes closed.

　「あなたには近くに海賊はいないのですか？」キムはたずねた。

　「いません！」美容師は叫んだ。「ひとりもいません！」。

　「まあ、それはお気の毒に。私にとって、人生でいちばん大切なのは神です。でも、その次に大切なのは常に海賊です」。

神様の次に大切なものは海賊デス

"Pirates never let you down, you know. Other people might, but not pirates. They stay with you to the end."

Then she eased open her eyes to find the beautician with her eyebrows barbed and an expression that begged a question.

"Don't you have any pirates near here?"

"No!" The woman shouted. "None at all!"

"Gee, that's too bad. As for me, I put God first in life. But next always come pirates."

ときに は、外国人たちは犯罪との関わり合いを告白することもある。その一例がこの男性である。彼は春の休暇をどう過ごしたかをたずねられたところだ。

「ああ、ぼくは監獄に2週間行ってたよ」。

「監獄!?」。

「うん、いい所だったよ。人々はとても親切だし、食物はうそみたいに美味しいときてるしね。君もいつか行ってみるといいよ」。

「いやあ」と、相手は反論した。「でもね、ぼくは一度も監獄に行きたいなんて思ったことはないけれど」。

「どうして？ソウルまでは飛行機で4万円もかからずに行けるのに」。

「ソウル？　韓国のことを言ってたの？」。

「そうだよ」と、彼は同意した。「そう言ったじゃないか、監獄って」。

別の外国人が告白した。「ぼくの趣味はスリです」。

彼が言葉を使いそこなったのは気の毒だった。彼はただ「ぼくの趣味は釣りです」と言いたかっただけなのに。

このちょっと気味の悪い話はどうだろうか。「みなさんに教えてあげます」と、ある外国人の教師が話し始めた。その教室いっぱいの生徒たちは、彼の流行遅れのネクタイのことでひやかしていたのだ。

「これはむかしわたしの祖父のネクタイだったのです」と、彼は言うつもりだった。

しかし、彼はネクタイの発音を間違えてしまった。

神様の次に大切なものは海賊デス

SOMETIMES foreigners will confess criminal involvement. An example is this man, who has just been asked how he spent his spring vacation.

"Oh, I went to jail for two weeks."

"Jail??"

"Yeah, and it was great. The people were so kind and food just fabulous. You should go sometime."

"Oh," his listener countered. "But I never want to go to jail!"

"Why not? A flight to Seoul costs hardly ¥20,000."

"Seoul? You mean South Korea? **Kankoku**?"   *Kankoku*

"Yeah," the man agreed. "Just what I said...**kangoku**."   *kangoku*

ANOTHER foreigner confesses: "My hobby is picking pockets."

Too bad he didn't use **tsuri** instead of **suri**. Then he would   *tsuri, suri*
have said "fishing."

OR how about this somewhat grisly tale from *Mangajin* magazine....

"I'll have you know," the foreign teacher begins. His roomful of students have been razzing him about his out-of-date necktie.

"That this was once my grandpa's tie."

Only the man errs on the word for necktie, a borrowed

「みなさんに教えてあげます。これはむかしわたしの祖父の肉体だったのです」。

さらに、別のおかしな外国人は「よやく」と「やく」を混同した。

彼は会議の席に突然とびこんできて、大声で言った。「みなさん、遅くなってすみません。でもわたしはホテルの部屋を焼かなきゃならなかったんですよ！」。

信じがたいことに、これよりもっとひどい乱暴なことも行なわれている。

「昨夜遅く」と、不精ひげのままの外国人は語学学校の同級生に告白した。「家内が女の赤ちゃんを埋めましたよ」。

たしかに「埋めました」は「生みました」に似ているが。

別の誇らしげなパパはあまりに疲れて授業に出る気になれず、一筆書いた。

「昨夜妻は４０００グラムの男の子を編みました。初めてのお産だったので、ちょっと大変だったようです。しかし、大した問題もなく、子供も元気です」。

ここでは「生みました」のかわりに「編みました」が使われている。

うわさによれば、後に彼の妻はさらに、一組の双子を含む３人の子供を「編んだ」そうである。

神様の次に大切なものは海賊デス

term pronounced in Japanese as **nekutai**. Instead he pronounces... **nikutai**.

nekutai
nikutai

"I'll have you know that this was once my grandpa's body."

YET, another wicked foreigner boo-booed on **yaku**—"to
burn"—and **yoyaku** to reserve.

yaku
yoyaku

He burst into a meeting and bellowed, "Sorry to be late
everyone, but I had to burn a hotel room!"

Incredibly, there is even worse mayhem afoot...

"LATE last night," the unshaven foreigner confesses to his
classmates in language school, "my wife buried a baby girl!"

With **umeru** meaning "to bury" and **umu** meaning "to
give birth."

umeru, umu

Another proud papa found himself too tired to attend
class, so he sent a note instead.

"Last night my wife knitted a four thousand gram boy.
It was a bit difficult as this was her first time, but there are
no major problems and the boy looks beautiful."

Here, in place of **umu**, the perverted verb is **amu**, "to
knit."

amu

Word has it, in fact, the wife later knitted three more kids,
including a set of twins.

さあ、この男はどうだろうか。彼はくっくっと笑いなが
ら、子供の頃友達と一緒によくやらかしたいたずらについ
て説明している。

　「ぼくたちはよく公園で女の子たちに近づいて行って、
彼女たちが油断しているすきをねらって、乳首に火をつけ
ものです。もちろん女の子たちはとび上がりましたよ！」。

　そうとうなワルだ。しかしながら、彼らが実際に火をつ
けたのは「乳首」ではなく「爆竹」だった。この種の言い
間違いの一因は、「彼女たちの」というような代名詞が、日
本語ではよく省かれるところにある。

　　　　　　　　　きわ　めて私的な事柄をあからさまにしてい
る告白もまた色々ある。

　「大学では何を勉強されたんですか？」と、採用担当者
が就職希望の外国人学生に聞いた。その学生は、たまたま
女性だったが、自信にみちた気取った笑みをうかべて答え
た。「勃起です」。いや、彼女は簿記と言ったつもりだった
のだが。

別のケースでは、ドイツ人のビジネスマンが札幌への旅行
について、やがて彼の姑となる日本人女性から聞かれた。

　「とても楽しい旅行でした。でも、思っていたよりずっ
と高くつきました。だって、一晩イッパツで４万円も払わ
されましたからね」。

　彼は「一泊」のつもりで「一発」と言ってしまった。こ
れがスラングで一回の性行為を意味することなど知る由も
なく。

神様の次に大切なものは海賊デス

OR how about this fellow, who giggles as he explains a prank he and his friends used to pull as boys.

"We used to get close to girls in the park, see, and then when they weren't watching, we would set fire to their nipples! Boy would they jump!"

Quite a prank at that. Except instead of **chikubi**—or "nipples"—he has intended **bakuchiku**—or "firecrackers," the flub made even easier by the fact that pronouns, such as "their," are often elided in Japanese.

chikubi
bakuchiku

OTHER confessions disclose intensely personal information.

"What did you study in college?" the employer asks his potential foreign hire.

Bokki, the woman tells him with a confident smirk, when she really means **boki**. In this latter, case, she studied "book-keeping." In the former, she studied "erections."

bokki
boki

IN another case, a German businessman was asked about his trip to Sapporo by his future Japanese mother-in-law

"It was great, but much more expensive than I imagined. Why, I had to pay ¥40,000 for a single night's stay!"

Except instead of "one night stay," **ippaku**, the man has used **ippatsu**. Which is Japanese slang for a single sexual act.

ippaku
ippatsu

似たような タイミングのまずさから、マシューの結婚式
でもしくじりが起きた。牧師が彼にこう聞いた。「あなた
は、この女性があなたの正式な妻であることを誓います
か?」このときマシューはしっかりとした声で言うべき
だった、「誓います!」と。

　声は大丈夫だった。問題は言葉だった。なぜなら、彼は
こう言ったのだ。

　「違います!」。

　これは「この女と結婚するのはいやだ!」という意味に
とれる。この言い間違いは、彼の内面の心理を映しだした
フロイト的窓と言えるかもしれない。

ある 会社で、若いガイジン女性が自分の体調を新しい上
司に伝えようとした。

　「早退した方がいいかと思っているんですが」片手をお
腹にあてて、彼女は説明しようとした。「行儀が悪いもの
ですから」。彼女は「行儀」と「具合」を間違えた。

次の 告白の舞台は日本語学校。嫌いなものをあげるよう
に言われたとき、そのクラスでいちばん温和な男子生徒が
叫んだ。

　「ぼくが嫌いなものは、クラスです!」。

　女教師は、その生徒は自分の教え方が気に入っている

神様の次に大切なものは海賊デス

A BLOTCH with similar bad timing occurred in Matthew's wedding. When the minister asked, "Do you take this woman to be your lawful wedded wife?" Matthew was supposed to say, in a firm voice, "**Chikaimasu**!" ("I so swear"). *chikaimasu*

The voice was no problem. The word was. For Matthew instead avowed:

"**Chigaimasu**!" *chigaimasu*

Which means "No way!"—a Freudian window to his inner self.

AT a business office a gaijin girl tried to express her own inner self to her new boss, but she bobbled the words for **guai** ("physical feelings")—and **gyôgi** ("manners"). *guai, gyôgi*

"I think I should go home early," she argued, pressing a hand to her stomach, "for I have bad manners!"

THE next confession, again from *Mangajin* magazine, comes at Japanese language school and hurts the teacher deeply. For when asked to express something he dislikes, the most gentle student in the room barked:

"Class!" In Japanese this is **kurasu**. *kurasu*

と思っていただけに、その告白を聞いてひどく心が傷ついた。その生徒が彼女の授業を気に入っているのは事実だった。彼にとって我慢ならないものは、東京の厄介者であるカラスだった。

ある 外国人は自分の気持ちを世間に向けて大声で言おうとしている。夜更けに、通りで若いカップルが話をしていた。フランクの寝室の窓からそう遠くない所に二人はいる。彼は眠れなかった。カップルはぺちゃくちゃとしゃべり続けている。

　　そこでフランクはベッドからはね起きて、窓をさっと開けた。そして叫んだ。「うれしい！」。

　実際は、彼は二度叫んだ。「うれしい！うれしい！」。カップルの耳にそれは奇妙に聞こえた。なぜなら彼は少しも嬉しそうには見えなかったから。フランクは「うれしい」と「うるさい」を間違えてしまったのだった…。

ここ にひとりの遅刻したビジネスマンがいる。彼は会議室にドアをバタンといわせながらとびこんで来て、大きな声で言った。「みなさん！ 失恋しました！」。

　「失恋」と「失礼」は発音が良く似ている。

神様の次に大切なものは海賊デス

And she thought the man liked her teaching!

Actually, he does. What the man can't stand is **karasu**   *karasu*
—or Tokyo's troublesome "crows."

MANGAJIN magazine now presents a foreigner eager to shout his feelings to the world.

It is late at night, and out on the street a young couple are talking—not so far from Frank's bedroom window. He can't sleep, and the couple keep gabbing and gabbing.

So he bounces up from bed, throws open the window and screams, "Shut up!"

In Japanese this comes out as one word: "**Urusai!**"   *urusai*

Except Frank blooped and instead yelled: "**Ureshii!**" In   *ureshii*
fact, he yelled it twice.

Resulting in the couple hearing the pajama-clad Frank bellow: "I'm happy! I'm happy!" Strange...because he didn't look happy.

NOW here's another late businessman, this time tripping over the phrase for "excuse me"—**shitsurei shimashita**   *shitsurei*
and a very similar sounding phrase—**shitsuren**
shimashita.   *shitsuren*

He slams into the meeting room and yells, "Everyone! I've lost my love!"

次の男はトレバー、彼は上記の男とは逆の問題をかかえている。

コンピューターおたくの彼は、会社ではずっと自分の小部屋に入りびたりである。彼は葦のごとく細く、幽霊みたいに青白く、そしていつも疲れているように見えた。彼が食べているところを誰も見たことがない。

「夕食はどうしてるの？」と、心配した同僚がたずねた。

「それは大丈夫」と、トレバーは答えた。「うちの近くのあちこちに恋人がいっぱいだからね。いつも何かはあるよ」。

この告白に同僚は黙ってしまった。これでトレバーがひどく疲れているわけがわかった。といっても、トレバーがあてにしているのは実は、恋人ではなくコンビニだったのだが。

神様の次に大切なものは海賊デス

THE next guy, Trevor, has the opposite problem.

A computer geek, he spends all his time in his office cubicle. He is as thin as a reed, as white as a ghost, and always looks worn down. No one ever sees him eat.

"What do you do for supper?" a concerned coworker asks.

"No problem," Trevor answers. "I've got lovers all around my house. They've always got something."

A confession which not only silences his coworker, but also helps explain why Trevor always looks so tired. Except that instead of lovers, or **koibito**, Trevor has meant **konbini**, or "convenience store."

koibito
konbini

　　ここで、第一章でふれた言い間違いのスターたちにもう一度登場願おう。「おこす」と「おかす」は、告白の中でも、伝説的な失言を引き起こしている。

　リックの会社での動きは午前中ずっと緩慢だった。両目の下にたるみができ、ときどきものすごく大きなあくびをする。ついに、同僚のひとりが聞いた。

　「リックさん、どうしたんです？　昨夜よく眠れなかったんですか？」。

　　彼の答え。「うん。家内とそのいまいましい寝返りのおかげでね。夜中に何度も何度も犯されちゃったよ」。

　おなじみの言い間違いスターの例はまだ他にも色々ある。これは「お尻」と「押し入れ」の場合。

　薬局のカウンターに心配顔の外国人が近づいて来た。店員の目には、その男性が頭の中で言うべき日本語をあれこれ考えているのが、見てとれた。彼はやっと話し始めたが、慎重な話し方をするものだから、一語一語に妙に力が入ってしまう。

　「ぼくの... お尻は... 嫌なにおいがします」それからその外国人は黙った。

　「確かですか？」と店員が言った。

　「確かですよ！」と外国人は答えた。「それを防ぐスプレーか何かありませんか？」。

　次に　紹介するのも、これもまたおなじみの言い間違いの例である。外国人たちが珍しい食生活を告白している。

　ある外国人女性が言った。「アメリカにいる頃、私は一

WE now move back to some blooper stars from chapter one—**okosu** and **okasu** (wake and rape)—in a confessional gaffe of legendary status.

okosu
okasu

All morning Rick has been dragging himself about the office. He shows bags under both eyes and now and then unwinds with an enormous yawn. Finally one of his co-workers asks:

"What's the matter, Rick-san? Didn't you sleep well last night?"

His answer: "No. Thanks to my wife and her blasted tossing and turning. I bet she raped me over a dozen times."

MORE old blooper stars, this time **oshiri** and **oshi-ire**, "butt" and "closet," respectively.

oshiri
oshi-ire

A troubled looking foreigner approaches the counter at a drugstore. The clerk can almost see the fellow aligning words in his head. When he at last speaks, the man does so deliberately, each word issued with practiced force.

"My...butt...stinks!" Then the foreigner pauses.

"Is that right?" says the clerk.

"Yes!" answers the foreigner. "Do you sell any spray for that?"

NEXT come even more old blooper friends, as foreigners now confess their unusual eating habits...

First **shiitake** (mushroom) and **shitagi** (underwear).

shitagi
shiitake

度も下着なんて食べたこと
がなかったけれど、日本では
いつも下着を食べているの
よ」。

　もちろん、次の質問は、
「誰の下着でもいいのです
か?」であろう。

「うんこ」と「あんこ」にも
再登場してもらおう。
　二人の外国人が語学学校
のお茶の時間におしゃべり
している。
　男A「僕はウンコの味がすごく好きなんだ」。
　男B「僕はいやだな。ちょっとがまんできないよ」。
　男A「へえ、でも駅の近くで新鮮なのを作ってる男を
　　　　知ってるよ。試してみるといい」。
　男B「僕が本当にいやなのは味じゃなくて、あの感触な
　　　　んだ」。
　この会話にはなんとなく食欲を削ぐものがないだろう
か。

「お腹 はすいていませんか?」と、日本人女性が自分の家
に滞在している外国人のひとりに聞いた。
　「いいえ、結構です。帰ってくる途中でハンドバッグを
食べましたから」。
　「ハンドバッグ」と「ハンバーガー」は発音が似ている。

神様の次に大切なものは海賊デス

The foreign woman says:

"I never ate underwear in the States, but here it's part of my regular diet."

Of course, the next question is, Will anyone's underwear do?

UNKO and **anko**— "poop" and "bean paste"—also take one more bow.   *unko*
anko

In this instance two foreigners talk during coffee break at language school.

Man A: I just love the taste of poop!

Man B: Not me. I can barely stand it.

Man A: Oh, but I know this guy down by the station who makes it fresh. You gotta try it.

Man B: It's not the taste that bothers me really; it's the texture.

Kind of ruins your appetite, doesn't it?

"HUNGRY?" asks a Japanese host of her foreign guest.

"No thanks. On my way here I ate a handbag."

With "handbag" being **handobaggu** and hamburger being **hanbâgâ**.   *handobaggu*
hanbâgâ

「お腹 はすいていませんか？」と、その女性は別の外国人客に聞いた。

　「いいえ、結構です。帰ってくる途中で祖母を食べましたから」。

　「祖母」と「蕎麦」も発音が似ている。

「お腹 はすいていませんか？」と、その女性は三番目の外国人客に聞いた。

　「いいえ、結構です。ちょうど今おいしいオチンコでごはんをいっぱい食べたばかりなので」。

　「オチンコ」と「おしんこ」も、まあ発音が似ている。とはいえ、食欲を減退させる言い間違いではある。

神様の次に大切なものは海賊デス

"HUNGRY?" asks the host to her next foreign guest.

"No thanks. On my way here I ate my grandma."

With grandma being **sobo** and buckwheat noodles be-   *sobo*
ing **soba**.   *soba*

"HUNGRY?" asks the host to guest number three.

"No thanks. I just ate a heaping bowl of rice with a delicious penis."

With penis being **ochinko**. **Oshinko**, on the other hand,   *ochinko*
is Japanese pickles....Talk about losing your appetite.   *oshinko*

　　　　　　　次にマイケルを紹介しよう。気品のある礼儀正しい男性だ。「お」を名詞の前につけると丁寧な表現になることを、彼は学んだばかりである。彼はみんなが色々な言葉に「お」をつけているのを、たえず耳にしていた。「おビール」とか「お尻」など。

　そのときマイケルは彼の日本人花嫁と並んで立っていた。花嫁に彼の同僚たちから称賛が浴びせられた。美しい、と彼らは彼女をほめたたえた。また、ファッションもすばらしいし、礼儀正しいとも言った。これほどまでにほめそやさられて、彼のとなりで花嫁は頬を染めていた。マイケルは自分も何か彼女のことをほめないといけない気がした。そして、彼女のお菓子作りの腕前をたたえることにした。

　「彼女のおパイはとてもおいしいんですよ！」と、彼はみんなに宣言した。

　これを聞いたマイケルの同僚たちは驚いて彼をじろじろ見た。そして花嫁は、新郎の足を蹴った。

「おっぱい」は「いっぱい」と発音が似ている。「いっぱい」は「満ちている」という意味だが、「満腹」を意味することもよくある。

神様の次に大切なものは海賊デス

AND now we introduce Michael, a gracious and mannerly fellow, who has just learned that sticking a little **o** on the front of nouns makes them honorific. He hears people doing this all the time, **obiiru** for "honorable beer," **oshiri** for "honorable butt," and so on.

At the moment Michael stands with his Japanese bride, basking in the praise showered upon her by his coworkers. She is lovely, his colleagues say. And so well dressed. And so

polite. So much that, with his wife turning crimson beside him, Michael feels obliged to add a compliment too and chooses to commend her baking.

"And her **o-pie**," he announces, "is just delicious!"   *o-pie*

Which earns him hands-on-mouth stares from his colleagues and a kick in the foot from his wife. For while Michael means "honorable pie," the word **oppai** is an-   *oppai*
other Japanese term for "breast."

OPPAI sounds similar to the word **ippai**. Meaning "full"   *ippai*
and often "full tummy."

"AHH!" sighs the full-bosomed foreign teacher. All the

　「ああ」と、胸の豊かな外国人の先生がため息をついた。
日本人教職員の全員が彼女の方に目を向けた。あたりには
空になった平皿や受け皿がある。この若い女教師の歓迎
パーティが行なわれている最中だった。
　「みなさん！」彼女は宣言した。「わたしはすっかりおな
かオッパイです！」。

似たような流儀で、外国人たちはそれぞれ自分が何者で
あるかを主張する。
　「わたしは田中さんの肛門です！」と、ある外国人が断
言した。これはよく知られている言い間違いで、「肛門」と
「顧問」との取りちがえである。

同様によく知られている別のミスの例。ジョンは自分の
アパートのドアのあたりに、女性がいるのを見つけた。彼
は、その女性が妻デビイの友人であることに気がついた。
しかしその女性の方は彼のことを知らなかった。
　「やあ、どうも」と、ジョンはアパートを背にして薄暗が
りから彼女にあいさつした。「わたしがデビイの囚人です」。
　「囚人」は「主人」と発音がまぎらわしい。ジョンが意
図したのは後者であったが。

「夫」をちょっと俗っぽく言うと「ひも」という言葉にな
るが、これには「ぐうたら男」のイメージがある。「ひも」
は「暇」と混同されがちだ。
　「ぼくは大体いつもヒモです」と、ボブが言った。
　すると、大勢の妻たちはつけ加えるかもしれない。
　「男ってみんなそうじゃない？」。

神様の次に大切なものは海賊デス

Japanese faculty swing to look her way. Around them lay the empty plates and saucers of the girl's welcome party.

"Everyone!" she announces. "I am a complete breast!"

IN similar fashion, foreigners claim to be many things...

"I am Mr. Tanaka's anus!" avers one foreigner in a error of much renown, inserting **kômon** for **komon**, the latter meaning "adviser." *kômon* *komon*

IN another mistake of equal fame, John peeps around his door to find a woman whom he recognizes as a friend of his wife's.

But the lady doesn't know him.

"Oh hi," he tells her from the gloom of the apartment behind. "I'm Debbie's prisoner."

Shûjin with **û** being prisoner and **shujin** with **u** being what John hopefully intended—"husband." *shûjin* *shujin*

A LESS savory word for husband is **himo**, which carries an image of a shiftless man. **Hima**, on the other hand, means "having free time." *himo* *hima*

"Most days," states Bob. "I'm a shiftless husband."

And many wives might add, "Aren't they all?"

さて、場面は会議が始まるところである。

　「アンダーソンさん！」鈴木氏が一礼して言った。「お元気ですか？」。アンダーソン氏も鈴木氏に一礼し、日本語で「お久しぶりです」とあいさつしようとした。ところが、そこでアンダーソン氏はヘマをしてしまった。結局、彼は元気よく言った。

　「やあ鈴木さん、オシボリです！」。

　場面はある教会へと移る。そこでは女性の全国大会が行なわれている。アメリカの婦人団体の代表として参加した来賓が紹介されているところだ。そのうちのひとりであるドローシーは日本語を少々知っていたので、来賓代表として話をすることになっていた。この日のために、彼女は何日も何日も練習してきた。ドローシーはマイクをとった。彼女のとなりに三人の友達が立っている。みな五十代後半の主婦である。ドローシーは着席している聴衆の方に視線を向け、姿勢を正し、そして話し始めた。しかし、あいにくなことに、彼女は言い間違いをしてしまった。それもなんという罪作りな言い間違いを…。

　「みなさん、こんにちは！ この大会に出席できて私はたいへん幸せです！」。

　その歯切れのよい日本語を聞いたとたんに、聴衆は感嘆の声をあげた。そして万雷の拍手。ドローシーはジュリア・ロバーツのようにほほえんだ。

神様の次に大切なものは海賊デス

NOW, we are at the start of a business meeting...

"Mr. Anderson!" schmoozes Mr. Suzuki with a bow. "How are you?"

Mr. Anderson bows back and returns the Japanese greeting for "It's been a while hasn't it?" This is **Ohisashiburi** desu.

ohisashiburi

Only he instead cracks off. "Ah, Suzuki-san! **Oshibori** desu!"

oshibori

With the full conversation being...

"Mr. Anderson! How are you?"

"Ah, Mr. Suzuki! I'm a wet towel!"

NOW we move to a church, one hosting a national convention for women. At the moment guests are being introduced from a women's group in the States. One of these guests, Dorothy, knows a bit of Japanese and has been selected to speak for the others. Dorothy has practiced her talk for days and days, but unfortunately shanks one of the first words she says. That being the word for "housewives" or **shufu**. Instead Dorothy says ....**shôfu**.

shufu
shôfu

She takes the microphone. Next to her stand her three friends, all housewives in their late fifties. Dorothy looks to the seated crowd, straightens and delivers...

"Hello, everyone! We are so happy to be here!"

At once come oohs of surprise at the sharp Japanese. Then a thunderclap of applause.

Dorothy smiles like Julia Roberts.

　「アメリカ本国の教会がみなさまへよろしくと申しております」。

　聴衆はドローシーの話を聞こうと静まりかえった。彼女がほほえみかけると、だれもがそれにこたえてにっこりとした。ところが、そのうちに意外なことを聞かされるのだ、聴衆のだれもが想像もしなかったようなことを…

　「わたしたちのアメリカの教会の会員の７０パーセント以上が女性で、その大部分がわたしたちと同じように…」ドローシーは傍らの友人を指した。「娼婦です！」。

　聴衆の顔からほほえみが消えた。だが、ドローシーはそれに気がつかなかった。そばにいる彼女の友人たちは、日本語もわからぬまま、同意を示すように小さく何度もうなずいている。それでドローシーは話の核心へと進んでいった。

　「娼婦として多忙ではございますが、それでもわたしたちは教会のための時間をちゃんとあけております。アメリカではみんなどこでもそのようにしています。それぞれの集会は勤勉な娼婦によって支えられているのです」。

　彼女は話をちょっと中断して、再びほほえんだ。「日本もまったく同じです。実際に、先ほどわたしは沢田牧師とお話させていただきましたが、牧師もご自分の教会が娼婦に負うところが多いことを認めていらっしゃいます」。

　このとき聴衆は沢田牧師の方を見た。牧師は元気のない笑みをうかべ、その目は必死に逃げ道を求めているように見えた。壇上でドローシーは話をしめくくった。

　「わたしたちはこの研修旅行中に、日本の娼婦のみなさんがどのように努力されているか、見学したく思っております。日本の状況をぜひ拝見させて下さい。わたしたちの

"I bring greetings to you from the church in the States."

The crowd settles in to listen, every single person returning Dorothy's smile. Only to then discover something none of them could imagine...

"Women make up over 70 percent of the membership in our U.S. church and most them are just like us...." Dorothy motions to her friends along side.

"Prostitutes!"

The crowd stops smiling. But Dorothy doesn't notice. Her friends beside her bob their heads with approval. So she spins on to the core of her speech.

"Even though busy prostitutes, we still find time for the church. That's how it is all across America. Each con-

言葉や文化は日本とは違っているとはいえ、わたしたちは
みなさんと共通の希望によって結ばれていることを確信し
ております。その希望とは、すべての人のために一層の努
力をすることです。ご清聴ありがとうございました！」。

　アメリカ人の一行は一礼した。半分に切ったパイほど
の大きなほほえみをうかべて。

　そして、日本人側もそれに応えて一礼した。アメリカ人
女性たちの派手な（tarty）ほほえみに比べると、彼女たち
の笑みは実に慎ましやかであった。

　（tarty には、「派手な」と「娼婦のような」という二重
の意味がある）。

これと同じ言い間違いの別の例。

　英語教師のアランは自分の担当授業のあらましを友だ
ちに話している。

　「でも、ぼくが好きなのは、水曜日午前の娼婦のクラス
なんだ。その娼婦たちはすごく愉快な人たちでね。ぼくの
他の生徒たちよりずっと経験豊富だし、とてもくつろいで
いる。あの娼婦たちの何人かが僕の夜のクラスに出席し
て、活気づけてくれるといいんだが。ところがね、きみも
知ってのとおり、その時間帯が娼婦たちはいちばん忙しい
んだよね」。

神様の次に大切なものは海賊デス

gregation backed by hardworking hookers."

She pauses to smile again. "Japan is surely the same. In fact, earlier I spoke with Pastor Sawada and he admitted his own church depends heavily on hookers."

At this moment the crowd turns to Pastor Sawada, who shows a sickly grin and eyes that search desperately for an escape.

On stage, Dorothy winds up.

"On this study tour, we are eager to see how Japanese prostitutes work. So please show us! Our language and culture may be different, but I know we are joined by a common desire to walk that extra mile for anyone. Thank you very much!"

The Americans bow, with smiles as wide as half-sliced pies.

And the Japanese bow back, their own smiles a lot less tarty.

MANGAJIN magazine offers a further idea on the same snafu.

Allan the English teacher has been outlining his work schedule for a friend.

"But my favorite lesson is my Wednesday morning hooker class. The hookers are so fun! They are so much more experienced than my other students and so relaxed! I wish a few of them would come and liven up my night classes, but, you know, that's when they're most busy."

次は 占い師の話。「あなたの星座は何ですか？」と、占い師がたずねた。

「星座？」と、外国人が言った。

「そうです。たとえば、わたしは双子座というように」

「ああ、それなら知っています！」この外国人の若い女性は自分の星座について聞いたことがあった。彼女は魚座だった。ところが、実際には彼女はこう言った。「わたしは餃子です！」。

お尻 が臭いと訴えるあの外国人男性を覚えておいでだろうか。さて、今度登場するのはおそらく彼の息子と思われる。この男の子ジミイは今日そわそわしている。九回目の誕生日をむかえたのだ。

　一般的に、「九」には「く」と「きゅう」の二通りの読み方がある。年令を表す接尾辞は「歳」である。この男の子の年令の正しい言い方は「きゅうさい」だ。「くさい」だって同様に理屈にあっていると思えるのだが、日本人は決してそうは言わない。というのは、そう言うと別の意味にとられるからだ。気の毒だが、小さなジミイはそれに気がついていなかった。

　「やあ、みんな当ててごらん。今日でぼくはクサイになったんだよ！」。

　真の悲報は、ジミイが向こう一年間ずっとクサイままだということだ。

神様の次に大切なものは海賊デス

NEXT off to a fortune-teller, in yet another blooper from *Mangajin* magazine. "What sign are you?" asks the medium.

"Sign?" the foreigner says.

"Yes. For example, I'm a Gemini."

"Oh I know!" The foreign girl has learned this before. "I'm a **uoza**!"   *uoza*

Which would have been perfect, for uoza is the Japanese term for Pisces with **uo** being "fish" and **za** in this case being "star."

Yet, the girl has actually said, "I'm a **gyôza**!"   *gyôza*

Which is a fried Chinese dumpling.

REMEMBER our foreign man with the smelly butt? Well perhaps this is his son, so excited today, his ninth birthday.

Now in Japanese there are two common ways to say nine, **ku** or **kyû**. The suffix designating age is **sai**. So the correct way to say nine years old would be **kyûsai**.   *kyûsai*

While **kusai** seems just as logical, no Japanese would   *kusai*
ever say this, for this word has another meaning. Too bad little Jimmy is not aware.

"Hey, everybody! Guess what! Today I stink!"

With the really bad news being he is going to continue that way for an entire year.

　　　　　　　話は ペニーへと移る。彼女は実に長い間人知れぬつらい悩みに耐えてきた。

　今日もまた、ペニーの一日はひどいものだった。いや、一週間ずっとひどかった。いや、生まれて以来ずっとだ。あるいは、少なくとも日本でのこの最後の年は。

　何をやってもうまくいかないように見えた。彼女は言葉、食物、そして仕事に四苦八苦していた。激しいカルチャーショックも味わった。それを克服しようとしてきたが、できなかった。彼女のあざやかなオレンジ色の髪、そばかすだらけの顔、それに６フィート１インチの身長が利点となることはなかった。同性は言うまでもなく、男性たちの９０パーセントは彼女より背が低いのである。

　どこに行っても、何をしても、彼女はいつも人にジロジロ見られるのを感じた。彼女がまるで動物園から逃げだした動物であるかのように。我慢しかねることが時々あった。実際のところ、彼女は感情が激発寸前なのを感じることが時折あった。ちょうど今のように。

　さて、ペニーは今、電車に乗っている。そばの席は空いたままだ。反対側にいる男性がスポーツ紙を読みながら、彼女をジロジロ見ている。そして、右側の吊り革につかまっている男子高校生は、彼女が身動きするたびに、視線を向けてくる。あるいは、彼女の席からひとつはなれたところに座っている主婦は用心深い、好奇心にあふれた目つきで、彼女を上から下まで見つめている。さらに、その主婦の三歳くらいの娘が、まるで無遠慮にぽかんとした目つきでペリーに見入っている。彼らはみな本日の無料ガイジンショーを見物しているのだ。

　ペニーはカーッとなった。あの男。あの少年。あの主婦。

神様の次に大切なものは海賊デス

BRINGING us to Penny, who had borne a silent burden for much too long.

As background, it must be noted that one Japanese character for people, **hito**, has the additional reading of **jin.** Another word, **ningen**, also means "people" or "person." Because of the meaning and sound, this second word is readily confused with still another word—**ninjin** ("carrot").

ningen

ninjin

Penny's day had been just terrible. No, her whole week had been terrible. No...her whole life.

Or at least this last year in Japan.

Nothing seemed to go right. She struggled with the language, with the food, with her job—severe culture shock that try as she might she could not sling off.

It did not help that she had bright orange hair, a face full of freckles and stood six foot one—taller than 90 percent of the men, let alone the women.

Wherever she went, no matter what she did, she always felt people staring at her as if she were a creature escaped from the zoo. Sometimes she could hardly bear it. Sometimes, in fact, she felt ready to explode.

Like right now.

Here she was on the train—with even a seat this time. But with the man across the way eyeing her over his sports paper and the high school boy on the commuter strap to the right flinging her looks whenever she moved. Or the housewife seated one space away, painting her up and down with cautious, curious eyes, and the

あの子供。みんなが彼女の赤毛と姿をジロジロ見ている。まるで彼女がカーニバルに現れる変な人であるかのように。

　ついに我慢できなくなった。

　その男がスポーツ紙のページをめくりながらペニーを見たときだ、彼女が完全にキレたのは。

　「わかったわ！」彼女は日本語で叫んだ。「もうわかったわよ！」彼女はいきなり立ち上がった。みんながとびあがった。乗客全員が彼女の方を向いた。

　「わたしはニンジンです、いいですか？　ニンジンなんです！よくごらんなさい。さあよく見て！」。

　みんな彼女の話を聞いてくれているようだった。みんな目を丸くしていた。

　「でも、みなさんにお知らせすることがあります。みなさんだってニンジンなんです！ひとり残らずそうなんですよ！」。今度は、彼女は指で指し始めた。最初はあの男。

神様の次に大切なものは海賊デス

woman's three-year-old daughter gawking at her with no reservations whatsoever. All of them soaking up tonight's free gaijin show.

It steamed her. The man. The boy. The housewife. The child. All staring at her red-headed figure as if she were a carnival freak.

Until she couldn't take it anymore!

The man lit her fuse by glancing up as he turned the page.

"All right!" she screamed in Japanese. "All right!" She popped to her feet.

Everyone jumped. The whole car turned to her.

"I'm a carrot, OK? A carrot! Take a good look, why don't you!!"

They looked all right. With eyes like saucers.

"But I've got news for you! You're carrots too! Every single one of you!"

Now she pointed. First, the man. "You're a carrot." Then the boy. "You're a carrot." Next, the housewife. "You're a carrot!"

Then she thrust her finger at the child. "And you're a little carrot too!"

The girl grabbed her mother's blouse. "Mama!" she cried.

The train rocked on, the passengers mesmerized by the livid foreigner.

"Don't you see?" Penny continued, gulping for air. "We're all carrots! So what does it matter if one carrot is tall or one carrot has red hair? Huh?"

「あなたはニンジンです！」それからあの少年。「あなたもニンジンです！」お次はあの主婦。「あなたもニンジンです！」それから、ペニーはあの子供に指を突きつけた。「そして、あなただって小さなニンジンです！」。

その小さな女の子は母親のブラウスにしがみついた。「お母さん！」女の子は泣きだした。

電車は走り続けた。乗客たちは、怒りで蒼白の外国人に唖然としていた。

「わからないのですか？」ペニーは大きく息をつくと、言葉を続けた。「わたしたちはみんなニンジンです！だから、あるニンジンが背が高くても、あるいは赤毛でも、何が問題だと言うのですか？」彼女は乗客たちを見回した。

「アメリカのニンジン、日本のニンジン、誰がそんなことを気にするでしょうか？ニンジンはニンジンなんですから。そうでしょう？」。

誰も答えなかった。身動きする者さえなかった。それで彼女はあの男子高校生の方を向いた。

「そうではありませんか？」。

高校生はたじろいで、その場をはなれようとした。

「わたしの言っていることは正しくありませんか？」彼女はどなった。

「正しいです」少年はどもりながら言った。「正しいです」。

ペニーはあのビジネスマンの方を向いた。「そして、あなたもそうです。ニンジンでしょう？」。

ビジネスマンはうなずいて言った。「そうです、私はニンジンです。ですから、まあ落ち着いて下さい」。

すみやかに乗客全員が体を震わせながら同意を示した。彼らは人参である。みんな平等にニンジンなのである。

神様の次に大切なものは海賊デス

She panned over the trainload of people.

"American carrots, Japanese carrots, who cares? We're still carrots! Right?"

No one answered her. No one even moved. So she swung to the high school boy.

"Right?"

He flinched and tried to step away.

"RIGHT!?" she hollered.

"Right," the boy stuttered. "Right."

She shifted to the businessman. "And you too! You're a carrot, right?"

The businessman nodded. "Yes, I'm a carrot. Just take it easy."

Pretty soon the entire car wobbled their agreement. They were carrots. All of them.

　ペニーは気持ちが落ち着いてくるのを感じた。怒りを爆発させたことで、気分がすっきりしたのである。何か素晴らしいことを成し遂げた気分で、彼女は元の自分の席にどっかと座った。人々はまだ彼女をじっと見ているが、どことなくそれまでとは違う目つきだ。たしかに、ビクビクした様子はまだ見える。おまけに、ほほえみをうかべているとはいえ、その目はあらぬ方を見ている。しかしながら、今では彼女に対する敬意が彼らの態度に感じられる。

　ペニーはみんなに大事なことを教えてあげた気分だった。そしてたぶん...必ずしも確実にとは言いがたいが...日本は彼女にとってそう住みにくい所ではなくなるだろう。

　もちろん、もしペニーが次に紹介する本章最後の外国人と同じくらい長く日本に住むことになったら、彼女はきっとカルチャーショックから脱することができるだろう。

「やあ、きみは日本語がうまいね」と、店主が言った。「どのくらい日本に住んでいるの？」。

　ほめられて、その外国人は気取った表情をうかべた...そして言い間違いの園へ足を踏み入れた。

　「ほんの 1000 年です」。

　この外国人は 1000 年ではなく、3 年と言いたかったのだ。

　しかし、もしかすると... 正しい日本語を習得するには、本当に 1000 年の年月が必要なのかもしれない。

神様の次に大切なものは海賊デス

Penny felt herself calming. The outburst had done her good. She flopped back in her seat, sensing she had accomplished something great. People still stared at her, but somehow with different eyes. Jittery eyes to be sure. Plus the smiles were cock-eyed. But now she sensed respect.

For she felt she had taught them something important. And maybe...just maybe...Japan would not be so hard for her anymore.

Of course, if Penny ends up staying in Japan as long as this chapter's final foreigner, she will probably outgrow her culture shock.

HEY, your Japanese is good," says the storekeeper. "How long have you lived here?"

The foreigner flicks back a smug expression—before pitching into Blooperland.

"Only a thousand years."

Mixing up **san** ("three") with **sen** "(thousand")."

san

sen

Though who knows... learning proper Japanese might truly take that long.

「貴男の妻と手を切りなさい！そうすれば天国は貴男のものです！」
説明や表現の仕方に関する言い間違い

　　　　　　　　ここまでの二つの章で扱った言い間違いの場合、そのほとんどは、不意打ち的なものであった。短い会話が一つの突然のチョンボのせいでいきなりギャグになってしまうパターンだ。

　しかしながら、これまで見てきたように、こうした会話の中には、ずっこけたまま先へどんどん進み、結果的に結構長めに続いてしまうものもある。話し手と聞き手の両者の間で、間抜けな言葉が続けてやりとりされるような、そんな拡張的な言い間違いを表す専門用語はこれだ。

　言いーーーーーーーーーーーーーーーー間違い！

神様の次に大切なものは海賊デス

GIVE UP YOUR WIVES, AND HEAVEN IS YOURS!

When explanations and presentations go bad

███████ MOST of the bloopers in the previous two chapters have been whip snaps—quick firecracks of conversation dominated by one booming bloop.

Yet, as we have seen, a handful of these conversations have rat-a-tatted on somewhat longer. The technical term for an extended blooper, in which both parties—speaker and listener—continue to volley the folly, is this:

Blooooooooooooooooper!

　　　　　　　　これから扱う日本語の言い間違いでは、特に長引くドジに焦点を当てている。まず、何かにつけて非常に長引く場所の一つと思われている場所、すなわち教会の礼拝の場から話は始まる。

　宣教師は在日外国人のなかで常に大きな位置を占めてきた。説教檀や街角、また教室などでしょっちゅう話をしているこうした日本在住の福音伝道者たちの多くは、実に正確な日本語の技能を身につけてきた。

　とは言っても、宣教師たちも伝説的な言い間違いをおかしており、それはほとんど神聖なほどである。

　以下に紹介するのは、これらの注目すべき言い誤りのいくつかを合成したもので、そのヘマのすべてが、ある特別な説教に詰め込まれている。

　ここに登場する架空の牧師をゲーリー・ベンキー師と呼ぶことにしよう。これはそう珍しい名前ではないが、誤解の種となる要素を多分に秘めている。

　なぜなら、「ゲーリー」を日本人が発音すると、それは「下痢」という言葉に危険なほど似ているからである。それに、「ベンキー」は「便器」を連想させる。多くのガイジンは、その職業を問わず、自分の名前が本来なら普通であるのに、日本人の耳にはバカげた派生的な意味を持つものとして聞こえることに気がつき、愕然とする。

　次に、ベンキー師を昔の時代へ置いてみよう。まだ日本にやって来る外国人も少なく、外国の生活についての情報も、あってもごくわずかという古い時代である。さて、外国のあらゆる事に関するうわさが当時とびかっていた。政治、教育、医学、そして宗教など。外国ではどんなことも可能であるように思え、純真な日本人はすぐにそれを信じ

神様の次に大切なものは海賊デス

OUR next foray into fractured Japanese focuses specifically on prolonged foul-ups. We begin in what some feel is one of the most prolonged places of all: a church service.

Missionaries have always accounted for a large segment of Japan's foreign population. Speaking regularly from pulpits, on street corners and in classrooms, many of these expat evangelists have developed surgically precise skills in Japanese.

Yet, they have also begat a share of bloopers so legendary they are almost holy.

The following re-creation is a composite of several of these noteworthy rimshots all packed into one special sermon.

Let's call our fictional minister, the Reverend Gary Behnke, a not-so-unusual name, but one with heavy blooper overtones.

For Japanese pronunciation of "Gary" sounds explosively close to the Japanese word for diarrhea — **geri** — *geri* and the word **benki** in Japanese means toilet bowl. Many *benki* gaijin of all professions have found themselves shackled by otherwise ordinary names which — to Japanese ears — have silly, secondary meanings.

Next, let's drop the Rev. Behnke back in time to a period when Japan yet had few foreign visitors and information about life in the outside world was scant at best. Hearsay ran rampant concerning all things foreign: politics, education, medicine — and religion. Overseas, it

た。このような純真な人々は、毎日外国人を見ることのできる横浜とか神戸といったにぎやかな港町よりは、むしろ田舎の活気のない山あいの谷間に多く見うけられた。

　こうした山あいの谷間の村にベンキー師は家を買ったばかりで、その家に人々を喜んで迎え入れた。信仰を広めようとはりきってあちこちとび歩いていたが、もっと日本語がうまく話せたらと思わずにはいられなかった。だが、彼の熱意はその欠点を補ってあまりあった。彼は物珍しそうな様子の聴衆の顔をじっとながめている。彼らは牧師の話を聞こうと集まった農民や職人である。やがて牧師はヘマの世界へ迷い込む羽目となる。

　ベンキー師は、単刀直入に話を始めるのがいちばん良いのだと、常々感じていた。

　「みなさんのうちで、何人の方が神の存在を信じていますか？」と、彼は大声を張り上げた。

　聴衆は彼をじっと見つめた。

　「さあ、神の存在を信じている方は手をあげて下さい！」。

　この敬虔な牧師は驚いた。なんと、その部屋にいたすべての人が、ひとり、またひとりと手をあげたのである。

　なぜみんな手をあげたのか。実を言うと、牧師は自分では気づかずに「神」という言葉を言いそこない、代わりに「亀」と言ってしまったのである。つまり、聴衆が実際に聞いた言葉は...

　「さあ、亀の存在を信じている方は手をあげて下さい！」。

　みんなが手をあげたのは、極めて当然と言えよう。

　「しめた！」と、牧師は聴衆のあげた手を見てほくそ笑んだ。「この土地を選んだのは大当たりだった！」こうなれば次のステップへ進むがよかろう...

　神様の次に大切なものは海賊デス

seemed, anything might be possible, with the most wide-eyed willingness to believe being found not in bustling Japanese port towns like Yokohama and Kobe—where people saw foreigners everyday—but rather in the sleepy mountain valleys of the Japanese countryside.

In one of which the Rev. Behnke has just purchased a house and welcomed in the public. He is hopping with excitement to share his faith and wishes he could speak Japanese better, but his enthusiasm more than makes up for his shortcomings. He peruses the curious crowd of farmers and craftsmen who have come to hear his talk… and then leaps into Blooperland.

The best start, he has always felt, is to be direct….

"How many of you," he cries, "believe in God?"

The crowd stares at him.

"Come now! If you believe in the existence of God, raise your hand!"

To the good Reverend's surprise, one by one each man in the room raises his hand.

For unknowingly Behnke has bumbled the word for god, **kami**. Instead, he has said, **kame**—which means *kami, kame* "turtle." As Japanese language typically needs no plural designations, the crowd has heard…

"If you believe in the existence of turtles, raise your hand!"

"Oh boy!" he titters, seeing the raised palms. "I've hit the jackpot!"

The next step…

　「では、みなさんのうちで、亀が唯一無二の存在と信じている方はいらっしゃいますか？ 偉大で全能な、唯一絶対の亀を信じている方は！」。

　村人たちはすぐにあげていた手をおろした。

　「うーむ、これはそう簡単にはいかないようだ」と、牧師は考えた。

　「ではみなさんに申し上げます。全世界で亀は唯一無二です！ 全世界で！」。

　一列目に座っていた男が、もじもじしながら言った。

　「でも、川には何十匹もいますよ」。

　「ああ、なんということだ！」牧師は口に手を当てた。「彼らは川の神の存在を信じている！」。

　「いいえ、亀は唯一無二なのです。亀は川とか山とか、あるいは海とかで区切られるものではありません。それにしても、みなさんはこの亀がそもそもなぜ特別なのかご存じでしょうか？」。

　村人たちは牧師を呆然と見つめた。彼が次に何を言う

神様の次に大切なものは海賊デス

"Now, how many of you believe that there is only one turtle? One great, almighty turtle!"

At once all the hands go down.

Uh oh, he thinks, perhaps it will not be so easy at that.

"I say to you that there is only one turtle for the entire world! For the entire universe!"

A man in the first row squirms in his seat. "But we have dozens down at the river!"

"Oh my gosh!" The Reverend covers his mouth. "They believe in river gods!"

"No! There is only one turtle! A turtle not limited by any river or mountain or sea. Yet, do you know what makes this turtle special?"

The men gape at him. They have no idea what he will say next.

"This great turtle loves people!"

A statement that would have been shocking enough.

のかまるで見当がつかなかった。

「この偉大な亀は、人間を愛するのです！」。

これだけでも十分ショッキングな発言であったに違いない。ところが、牧師は二重にヘマをしてしまった。「人間」と「人参」も取りちがえたのだ。

「この偉大な亀はニンジンを愛するのです！ みなさんはそれを信じますか？」。

数人がうなずいた。まあ、そういうこともありうるだろう。

「亀は何よりもニンジンを愛するのです。信じますか？」。今度は聴衆に指先を突きつけた。

「はい、信じます」と、ひとりの村人が言った。

ベンキー師は何度も何度も指先を向け、前の方の席に座っていた男たちから言質を求めた。その度に肯定的な反応を得た。亀は人参が大好きかもしれないと、みんなが同意してくれた。

「わたしは偉大な福音伝道者ではあるまいか」と、牧師はひとりごとを言った。そして、彼は話の核心へと迫っていった…

「偉大な亀はニンジンを愛するあまりに、御自分の一人息子をニンジンに与えることさえいとわないのです！」。

これを聞いて、聴衆はみんなびっくり仰天した。なんだって！？

「飢えてる亀の子供に人参なんて聞いたことねえずら」。と、後ろの方に座っていた男がつぶやいた。

ベンキーは、あまりに多くのことを急いで話してしまった誤りに気づき、話の調子を変えることにした。

「神はみなさんのひとりひとりに約束を作りました！」。

神様の次に大切なものは海賊デス

Yet, again the Reverend blooped, this time switching **ningen** and **ninjin**. This, as we have already seen, is a trade of "person" or "people" for "carrots."

ningen
ninjin

"This great turtle loves carrots! Do you believe it!?"

A few men nod their heads. Yes, it seems plausible.

"This turtle loves carrots more than anything! Do you believe!?" This time he aims a finger into the crowd.

"Yes," a man says. "I believe."

Again and again the Rev. Behnke points and seeks commitment from the men up front, always to be met with a positive response. Everyone agrees that a turtle might love carrots.

"Am I a great evangelist or what?" hums the Reverend to himself. Now he moves to the heart of the matter...

"This great turtle loves carrots so much it is willing to give it's only son for them!"

The people startle at this. Inconceivable!

"I can't imagine anything that hungry," mutters a man

　"Make a promise"の意味の日本語としてはややぎこちないが、まあ言いたいことは分かる。もし正しく言えてさえいれば。だが実際には、牧師は「約束」という言葉も言い間違えた。彼はこう説いた...

　「亀はみなさんひとりひとりに焼そばを作りました！」。村人たちはさらにひどく仰天した。

　「この焼そばは決してなくなることはありません、どんなことがあろうと！」牧師は叫んだ。

　「この宗教はおれに合ってるかもしれないな」と、村人のひとりがささやいた。

　「亀はみなさんと共に在り、みなさんにとても大きな望みを与えてくれます！」…と言うはずだったのに、ここでもまた牧師はミスった。今度言いそこなった言葉は「望み」である。

　「亀はみなさんと共に在り、みなさんにとても大きなネズミを与えてくれます！」。

　これを聞くと、村人たちのあいだにざわめきが起こった。というのも、ここの農民たちにとって、この世でいちばん不要なものがネズミだったからである。数人が帰ろうとして立ち上がった。

　「ああ、帰らないで下さい！」ベンキー師は聴衆が立ち去ろうとしているのを見て、とっさに方向転換をした。「待って下さい！もし罪と手を切れば、みなさんは全員天国へ行くことができます」。

　この言葉で村人は出ていくのをやめた。もう一度話を聞くために、腰をおろした。みなはその先が知りたくてたまらない。

　ベンキー師はほっとした。彼は気づいていなかった。村

神様の次に大切なものは海賊デス

in the back.

Behnke senses he has poured on too much too fast and changes gears.

"The turtle has made you each a promise!"

Yet now the Reverend has mixed up the word for promise **yakusoku** and has instead preached... *yakusoku*

"The turtle has made you each fried noodles!" With

yakisoba being a well-known noodle dish in Japan. *yakisoba*

The people are now even more startled.

"And these noodles will never go away, no matter what!"

"I might like this religion," whispers one.

"The turtle will stay with you and give you tremendous hope!"

Now the blooped word is "hope." For instead of **nozomi** the man of the cloth has said, "**nezumi**!" *nozomi*

"The turtle will stay with you and give you tremen- *nezumi* dous mice!"

人たちに「罪」のつ
もりで「妻」と手を
切ることで天国へ
行けると言ってし
まったことに。

　「そうです、妻と
手を切りなさい！
そうすれば、天国
はみなさんのもの
です！」。

　男たちが話に耳を傾けてくれているうちに、お祈りの
時間をとった方がいい、と牧師は判断した。

　「みなさん、目をつぶって下さい」。

　だがベンキー師は「つぶって」と言うべきところを「つ
ぶして」と言った。

　「みなさん、目をつぶして下さい！」。

　牧師は頭を下げ、大声で言った。「神よ、どうか私たち
の魂に救いの手をさしのべ、解放し給え！」。

　ところが、牧師が実際に言った言葉は「解放」ではなく
「解剖」だった。

　決してなくならない焼そばと見捨てられた妻を織りまぜ
た牧師の祈りは、長ったらしさと真情にあふれていた。彼
は自分自身の言葉にすっかり没頭していたから、やっと我
に返り、目を開けたときには...部屋はもう空っぽだった。

　しかし、ベンキー師はあきらめるような男ではなかった。
というのは、他の多くの宣教師たちと同様に、彼の心は「ネ
ズミ」ならぬ「望み」で満ちあふれていたからである。それ
は村人みんなと分ち合えるくらい満ちあふれていた。

神様の次に大切なものは海賊デス

This causes considerable mumbling—because the last thing these farmers need is mice. Several rise to leave.

"Oh no!" The Rev. Behnke sees he is losing his audience and springs in another direction. "Wait! You can all enter into heaven if you just give up your sins!"

This stops the exodus. Once more the men settle down to listen, eager to learn more.

The Rev. Behnke relaxes, not knowing he has told the men they can get to heaven by giving up their **tsuma**, when he really meant **tsumi**. Tsuma means "wife." *tsuma* *tsumi*

"Yes! Give up your wives! And heaven is yours!"

Time for prayer, he decides, while he has their attention.

"Close your eyes everyone!"

Only the command form of the verb to close one's eyes is **tsubutte**. Behnke has instead used **tsubushite**. *tsubutte* *tsubushite*

"Crush your eyes everyone!"

He bows his head and bellows: "Turtle! Please take our spirits and free them!"

Kaiho means "to free" while **kaibo**, the Reverend's term, means "to perform an autopsy." *kaiho, kaibo*

Packed with never-ending noodles and abandoned wives—the Reverend's prayer is both windy and heartfelt. He dives deep into his own words and when he finally comes up and uncrushes his eyes...he finds the room empty.

Yet he is not a fellow to quit. For, like many missionaries, he is a man brimming with mice. Enough to share with everyone.

キリスト教 が日本で長年にわたって果たしている役どころのひとつに、西洋風結婚式の提供がある。これは、日本人でさえもウェディングドレスや教会の鐘に対してロマンティックな夢を抱いているからである。その結果として、宣教師たちが沢山のこうした儀式をとり行ない、そして…沢山のヘマもやらかす。

　「さあ」と、牧師が出席者たちに言った。新郎新婦は彼の前にさっそうと立っていた。「新郎新婦は性欲を取り交わします！」。

　牧師が言わんとしたのは「性欲」ではなく「誓約」だったのだが。

　それから牧師は新郎にたずねた。「汝はこの女性を汝の罪として受け入れますか？」。

　この言い間違いは前述のベンキー師のそれに似ている。

　今度は新婦にたずねた。「そして、汝はこの男性を汝の嘔吐として受け入れますか？」。

　言うべき言葉は「嘔吐」ではなく「夫」である。

　最後に待ちうけている落し穴がある。実はこれはもっともよく知られている言い間違いのひとつなのである。

　誓約が終了し、牧師は両手を新郎新婦の頭上にかざして高らかに唱えた。「汝ら二人に、神の永遠の復讐がありますように！」。

　かわいそうな夫婦。牧師が「祝福」と「復讐」を取り違えたばかりに…。

　神様の次に大切なものは海賊デス

THROUGH the years, one niche Christianity has found in Japan is as a provider of Western-style weddings. For even Japanese are smitten with romantic visions of bridal gowns and church bells. Consequently, missionaries perform lots of such ceremonies...and make lots of bloopers as well.

"And now," the minister announces to the crowd, with the new couple standing smartly before him. "The bride and groom will exchange their lust!"

Seiyoku meaning "lust" and **seiyaku** meaning "wedding vows." *seiyoku seiyaku*

"Do you," the minister then questions the groom. "Accept this woman as your sin?"

Pulling a boner similiar to the Rev. Behnke's.

"And do you," the minister now asks the bride. "Accept this man as your vomit?"

"Vomit" being **oto** and "husband" being **otto**. *oto, otto*

Then, the kicker, one of the most well-known language bloopers of them all...

Vows completed, the minister raises his hands over the newlyweds and pronounces: "May God's blessings be on you forever!"

With blessing being **shukufuku**. But if you goof and instead cry "**fukushû**," it comes out... *shukufuku fukushû*

"May God's vengeance be on you forever!"

　　　　　　　　ここで 話題を宗教から健康へと変えて、新
婚カップルのヒロとテリーを訪ねてみよう。

　結婚まもないヒロが病気になった。こんなことは、結婚
前の恋愛期間中にもなかったことである。もうすでに会社
を一日欠勤してしまった。明日もきっと休む羽目になりそ
うである。

　テリーは、夫がそんなにつらそうな様子をしているの
を、今までに一度も見たことがなかった。彼は部屋着のま
まで、こたつにもたれるようにしている。ティッシュで鼻
は赤むけの状態、目は涙ぐんでいるようで白っぽい、顔全
体にしまりがなく、腫れぼったい感じだった。数分おきに
ひびわれた唇をなめ、のどをごくりとさせてはしかめ面を
する。そんな様子を見ているのさえ胸が痛んだ。

　テリーはこたつ板の上に、湯気をたてている茶わんを
置いた。「さあ」と彼女はなだめるように言った。「これを
飲んでみてよ。きっと効くと思うわ」。

　彼は身動きせずに言った。「それ、何なの？」。

　「おばあちゃんゆずりの家庭用風邪薬なの。効き目は保
証つきよ」。

　「中に何が入っているの？」と、彼はたずねた。

　「とにかく飲んでみてよ。さめないうちにね。そうした
ら中身を教えてあげる」。

　彼はじっとしたままだった。

　「ヒロったら！あなたは風邪を治したいの？それとも治
したくないの？」。

　「わかった、わかったよ」妻に日本語でキーキーどなら
れるのがヒロはいちばん苦手だった。

　彼はその茶わんを口元にもっていき、すすり始めた。

神様の次に大切なものは海賊デス

SHIFTING from religion to health, we now visit the newlyweds Hiro and Terri...

For the first time in their courtship and young marriage, Hiro had taken ill. He had already missed one day at the office and would certainly be absent the next day too.

Terri had never seen him look so miserable. He sat reclining at the **kotatsu** in his bathrobe, his nose pink from having been rubbed raw with tissues, his eyes watery and blanched, and his whole face slack and nubbled. Every few minutes he would smack his cracked lips and grimace as he swallowed. It ached even to watch him.

She sat the steaming cup on the tabletop. "Here," she coaxed. "Drink this down. It'll help."

Hiro didn't move. "What is it?"

"My grandmother's home cold remedy. Guaranteed to work."

"What's in it?" he asked.

"Just drink it before it gets cold. Then I'll tell you."

He still didn't move.

"Hiro! Do you want to get better or not?!"

"OK, OK!" The last thing he needed was his wife's hollering in her squeaky Japanese.

He brought the cup to his lips and began to sip... Dark tea, spiked and sweetened.

"Don't sip it! Drink it fast! That's part of the cure."

So he opened his mouth and welcomed the hot liquid down his tortured throat. He took four gulps, five, then paused for breath—to see Terri smiling at him like a little

黒っぽい紅茶で、アルコールが入っており、甘味をつけて
ある。

「チビチビ飲むんじゃだめ！ 一気に飲まなきゃ！ 飲み
方も効き目に影響するんだから」。

そう言われて、彼は口をあけ、ひりひりとするのどにそ
の熱い液体を迎え入れた。4回飲み込んだ。そして5回
目。それから一息ついて見ると、テリーは看護婦さんごっ
こをしている少女のように、彼の方を見てほほえんでい
た。彼はさらに3回飲み込んで、やっと飲み干した。彼は
茶わんを置いた。

「ほーらね、そうまずくもなかったでしょう？」。

「うん」しかし、当然のことながら、彼には味などほと
んどわからなかった。「何が入っていたの？」。

「当ててみてよ」。

「テリー、あのねえ、ぼくは気分が悪いんだぜ」。

「んもう、しらけるわねえ。まあいいわ。まず、ブラッ
ク・ティー(完全発酵させた黒っぽい紅茶)だったことはわ
かったわよね？」。

「うん」。

「ブランデーが二滴ほど入っているのよ」。

ヒロにもそのくらいの見当はついた。

「それからレモンの厚切りを一枚しぼって入れたの」。

「げー」。

「最後に秘密の材料を加えるのよ。何だと思う？」。

「テリー…」。

「さあ、当ててごらんなさい」。

「テリー、たのむよ、ぼくは気分がよくないんだ」。

そうして、彼は若い妻のドジのおかげでいっそう気分

神様の次に大切なものは海賊デス

girl playing nurse. Three gulps more and he was finished. He set down the cup.

"There. That wasn't so bad, was it?"

"No." But, of course, he could barely taste a thing. "What was in it?"

"You gotta guess."

"Terri, come on. I feel awful."

"OK, spoilsport. First, it's just black tea, right?"

"Right."

"Laced with two shots of brandy."

He figured as much.

"Then I squeezed in a fat slice of lemon."

"Yuck."

"Last comes the secret ingredient. Can you guess what?"

"Terri..."

"Come on, guess."

"Terri...No. I don't feel well."

And then he felt even worse as his young wife blooped, switching the word for honey—**hachimitsu**—with the word **hanamizu**.

hachimitsu

hanamizu

"Well, it's a spoonful of snot."

Hiro jumped. "What?"

"See. You feel better already."

"You put snot in there?"

"Right. That's Grandma's secret ingredient. A tablespoon of snot mixed with brandy and lemon and served piping hot. 'It'll either cure you or kill you,' she always said."

が悪くなった。

「まあいいわ、それはね、スプーン一杯の鼻水よ」。

ヒロは飛び上がらんばかりに驚いた。「なんだって！？」。

「あら、早くも効き目が現れてきたみたいね」。

「きみはあの風邪薬に鼻水を入れたの？」。

テリーが実際に入れたのは「鼻水」ではなく「蜂蜜」だった。しかし彼女は自分の言い間違いに気づかない。

「そうよ。おばあちゃん直伝の秘密の材料ですもの。ブランデーとレモンにスプーン一杯の鼻水を混ぜて、熱々のうちに出すのよ。『すっかり治ってしまうか、あるいは逆にひどくなるかのどちらかだよ』って、おばあちゃんがいつもそう言っていたわ」。

ヒロはあわててティッシュを取って、口をぬぐい始めた。

「あなたの場合、わたしはあなたをとても愛しているから、二杯入れたの。確かに効き目があるようにね」。

ヒロはティッシュに吐き出した。ティッシュ越しに妻の顔を盗み見ると、彼女は愛情に満ちあふれた表情をしている。

「さあ、本当のことを言って」彼女は目を輝かせて言った。「わたしと結婚してよかったと思わない？」。

次の カップルの間でも、似たような言い間違いが起こっているが、これもやはり、あまりありがたくないものがからんでいる。このカップルはまだ結婚していない。男性の方は結婚にこぎつけようとしているのだが。

たとえば、今夜テッドは手作りの食事をごちそうしよ

Hiro grabbed a tissue and started wiping his mouth.

"In your case, since I love you so much, I put in two tablespoons, just to be sure."

Hiro hacked into the tissue, over which he spied his wife's adoring face.

"Now...tell the truth," she gleamed. "Aren't you glad you married me?"

WITH our next couple, we encounter a similar blunder with another detestable substance. In this case, the couple are not yet married, though the fellow is working on it.

Tonight, for example, Ted has invited Keiko to his

うと、圭子を自分のアパートに招待した。強烈な印象を与えたくて、彼はキャンドルライト、静かな音楽、そして一本のワインを用意した。さらに、彼はもっとすてきなものをつけ加えた。ブロッコリーとチキンのキャセロールだ。彼は母親からいろいろな料理を伝授されたが、これはその中のひとつである。

　一方、圭子は幾分緊張気味だった。今まで男性のアパートを訪れたことなど一度もなかったし、外国人の場合は言うまでもない。それに、彼女は海外へ行った経験がまるでなかった。今、彼女はテッドのアメリカ風のアパートにきている。座って、これまで一度も味わったことのない料理を食べているところだが、まるで別世界にやってきたような気分である。

　実際のところ、別世界というのは当たっている。といってもアメリカではない。圭子はまもなく発見するだろう、言い間違いの国にやってきてしまったことを。

　そのキャセロールはおいしく、圭子は気に入った。テッドはそれに気がつき、彼女におかわりをすすめた。彼女は料理を皿にとりわけて、そのおいしさを一口味わった。

　「あなたがこれを作ったなんて信じられないわ。とてもおいしいんですもの」。

　「いやあ、こんなのは簡単な料理だもの」謙虚であろうとして、テッドは言った。「おふくろのやり方をまねただけさ」。

　「何が入っているの？」。

　「わからない？」。

　チキン、ブロッコリー、チーズ、ホワイトソース。圭子は簡単に主要な材料をあげることができた。

神様の次に大切なものは海賊デス

apartment for a home-cooked meal. He hopes to make a big impression, with candlelight, soft music, a bottle of wine and one of his mother's more fabulous recipes—broccoli and chicken casserole.

Keiko, meanwhile, is a bit nervous. She has never been to a guy's apartment before, let alone a foreigner's. She has never been abroad before either. Now, sitting in Ted's American-style dwelling and eating food she has never tasted, she feels she has entered another world.

And indeed she has. But rather than America, Keiko will soon discover that she has arrived in Blooperland.

The casserole tastes good. Keiko likes it.

Ted notices and offers her more. She dishes up another spoonful and takes a dainty bite.

"I can't believe you made this. It's so delicious."

"Oh it was a snap," Ted says, trying to be modest. "I just followed my mom's directions."

"What's in it?"

"Can't you tell?"

Chicken, broccoli, cheese, white sauce: Keiko has no trouble listing the main ingredients.

"Yeah, but there's one more thing that makes the flavor special. Any idea?"

She shakes her head. The food, the wine, Ted's easy manners—she is starting to relax.

"OK, I'll tell you." He raises his brows. "It's **gomi**."   *gomi*

Keiko rocks back. "Gomi?!"

Not knowing that Ted does not mean gomi but rather

「その通り。でももうひとつあるんだ。それが独特の風味をつけているんだけどね。何だかわかる？」。

圭子は首を横にふった。この料理、ワイン、それにテッドの打ち解けた態度... 彼女の緊張もだんだんほぐれてきた。

「よし、教えてあげよう」彼は眉をあげた。「それはゴミなんだ」。

圭子は驚いた。「ゴミ！？」。

テッドが意図した言葉は「ゴミ」ではなく「胡麻」だったのだが、圭子はそれに気づかなかった。ゴミと胡麻はかなり違う。テッドの言葉によると...

「そうなんだ。あるゴミを混ぜたんだ。たくさんのゴミをね。これがちょっとした歯ざわりを添えていると思うんだけれど」。

圭子はフォークを置いた。彼女の皿には、半分食べかけた料理がのっている。目をぱちくりさせて、それを見た。

「ゴミなの？」首をのばして彼女はまた聞いた。テッドはうなずき、話を続けた。

「でも、どこにでもあるようなゴミじゃないよ。僕が使ったのは特別なゴミで、おふくろがはるばるボストンから送ってくれたものなんだ。船便で六週間かかって、昨日届いた。ギリギリで間に合ったんだよ」。

圭子はまた目をぱちくりさせて自分の皿を見た。テッドは食べるようにすすめる。

「さあ、遠慮しないで。全部きみのために作ったんだから！」。

神様の次に大切なものは海賊デス

goma, which is "sesame seed." Gomi, on the other hand, *goma*
is Japanese for something very different. In Ted's words...

"Yep, I mixed in some garbage. Lots of it. It adds a
certain crunchiness, I think."

Keiko sets down her fork. She blinks at the half-eaten
helping on her plate.

"Garbage?" she asks again with her neck extended. Ted
nods and continues.

"But not just any garbage. I used special garbage that
my mom sent all the way from Boston. Six weeks by ship
and it arrived yesterday, just in time."

Keiko again blinks at her plate, while Ted urges:

"Don't be shy now. It's all for you!"

ひょっとすると、テッドは語学学校で次のような発表をした生徒と同一人物かもしれない。その生徒の話の題目は「日本の折紙」と記載されている。

　「今日、わたしは日本の美しい伝統的な折りゴミについて、お話をしたいと思います。まずはじめに、折りゴミの歴史についてちょっとお話をして、それからみなさんに簡単な折りゴミのやり方をお教えしようと思います。日本の方たちがやっているのとまったく同じ折り方です」。

次の 発表をした学生の場合、第一章で紹介したデビッドと同じ間違いをしている。つまり、「お寺」と「お手洗い」の混同である。この学生の話の題目は「お寺」だが、彼はこんな風に始めた。

　「お手洗いは日本のいたる所にあります。昔の日本人の生活では重要な位置を占めていたのですが、今日ではお手洗いは観光名所も同然です。現代の日本人の中で、お手洗いを定期的に訪れる人はほとんどありません。それに、一度もお手洗いに行ったことのない人たちさえいます。もちろん、亡くなった人に別れを告げる場合は別ですが」。

次の 若い女性も同様に表現の仕方で失敗した。メアリーの場合、話をした場所は語学学校ではなく、自分の教会だった。彼女は、教会へやってくる人たちに、クリスマスイブの礼拝にどう参加すればいいかを案内しようとした。

　「おいでになるときに」と、メアリーは言った。「みなさんがそれぞれ冷蔵庫をお持ち下さるとよろしいかと思いますが」。

　「冷蔵庫ですって？」。

神様の次に大切なものは海賊デス

WHO knows, Ted may have also been the fellow who made the following presentation in language class. His listed topic: Japanese **origami**...or "paper-folding."   *origami*

"Today, I want to talk about the beautiful and traditional Japanese art of garbage folding. First, I am going to say a few words about the history of this craft, then I'm going to teach you all how to do some simple garbage folding, just like the Japanese."

THE student with the next presentation then made the same mistake as David in Chapter one, confusing the words **otera** and **otearai**—temple and toilet. His talk was   *otera*
on "temples" and here is how he began...   *otearai*

"Toilets can be found all across Japan. Although an important part of Japanese life in years gone by, today they are little more than tourist spots. Very few modern Japanese visit them regularly and some never go there ever—except of course to bid farewell to their dead."

THE next girl, in another story from *Mangajin*, is equally unsuccessful in her presentation. In Mary's case, she is speaking not at language school but at her church. She is trying to inform some visitors how they can participate in the Christmas Eve service.

"When you come," Mary says, "It would be a good idea if you each bring a refrigerator."

"Refrigerator!"

　「ええ」と、メアリーは説明した。「礼拝のあとで、私た
ちは冷蔵庫に火をつけます。それから冷蔵庫を持って、家
から家へクリスマスキャロルを合唱して回るんです」。
　もちろん、メアリーが意味したのは「冷蔵庫」ではなく
「ロウソク」である。これなら、運ぶのもさほど大変では
ない。

　一方、この家電製品が惨事を招くことは珍しくもないよう
だ。カールがどのように前の晩の嵐を説明するかを見てい
ただきたい。
　「それから、ものすごい雷鳴がして、家の明かりが全部
消えてしまいました。懐中電灯がなかったので、僕は次善
の策をとりました。ライターを引っ張り出してきて、冷蔵
庫に火をつけました。ありがたいことに、冷蔵庫はゆっく

神様の次に大切なものは海賊デス

"Yes," Mary explains. "After the service we will light them up and carry them with us as we go Christmas carolling."

Of course, Mary meant **rôsoku** or "candles" and not the much harder to carry **reizôko**.

rôsoku
reizôko

On the other hand, hardware infernos of this sort might be common. Witness Carl's description of last night's storm.

"Then with this one enormous crack of thunder, my lights went out. I didn't have a flashlight, so I did the next best thing. I tugged out my cigarette lighter and set fire to my fridge. Thank goodness it burned slowly, as the lights didn't return for over an hour."

At least he didn't get lost in the dark. Next is a guy who got lost in broad daylight.

FOR this fractured tale we introduce **unchi**, yet another Japanese word for "poop." In this case, unchi has been confused with **uchi**—the word for house.

unchi
uchi

The man tells one friend about another:

"I hunted for Hank's poop for over an hour yesterday. Up and down every street. I thought I had it once, but it turned out to be some other guy's."

り燃えてくれました。明かりが再びついたのは、一時間以上もたってからです」。

　少なくとも、カールは暗闇で途方に暮れることはまぬがれた。次に登場する男性の場合は、真昼間なのに迷ってしまった。その男はある友人と、ハンクという名の別の友人について話をしているところである。

　「ぼくは昨日一時間以上もかけてハンクのうんちをさがしたよ。あらゆる通りをあちこちさがしたんだ。一度は彼のうんちを見つけたと思ったんだけれど、結局は別人のうんちだった」。

　「それで、どうしたの？」友人がいぶかしそうに聞いた。

　「ええと、ぼくはそこの人に聞いたんだ。この近所にうんちをもっている外国人を知っていますかって。でもその人はぼくをにらみつけただけで、ドアをしめてしまった」。

　「うんち」と「うち」の、ささやかな言い間違いに過ぎなかったのだが。

　　　　　　　　ここで　話題は途方にくれた外国人から、持ち物をなくしてしまった外国人へと変わる。

　浜辺でうたた寝をしていたアンディは、目をさますと財布がなくなっているのに気がついた。それで、彼は町まで歩いて行き、交番をさがした。

　アンディはこう言おうとした。「僕の財布が見つからないんです！」。

　実際には、アンディはこう言った。「僕の制服が見つからないんです！」。

　彼は財布と制服を完全に勘違いして覚えていた。すると、

神様の次に大切なものは海賊デス

"What did you do?" his friend wonders.

"Well, I asked the guy if he knew any foreigner with poop in the area. But the man just glared at me and closed the door."

NOW we move from lost foreigners to foreigners who lose things.

After a nap on the beach, Andy wakes up to discover his wallet is missing. So he treks into town to find a police box.

What Andy wished to say: I can't find my wallet! (The word for wallet being **saifu**).   *saifu*

What Andy actually said: I can't find my uniform! (Which is **seifuku**).   *seifuku*

"OK, OK, take it easy," the cop on duty tells him. "Let

　「わかりました、わかりました、そう興奮しないで」と、当直の警官がアンディに言った。「報告書を書かせて下さい。きっと出てきますよ。さて、あなたがそれを最後に見たのはどこでですか？」。

　「浜辺です。ぼくの他の持ち物と一緒に置いてあったんですが」。

　アンディの言葉をくり返しながら、警官は報告書に鉛筆で記入した。「浜辺... で、それはどんな種類ですか？」。

　どんな種類？「えーと... 色は茶色で全体が革製です」。

　「茶色で全体が革...」ここで警官は口をつぐんだ。彼は机からアンディをじっと見つめた。「全革製の制服を一体どうするんです？」。

　アンディはいらいらしてきた。「どうする？ それじゃああなたは、ぼくが制服をどうすると考えているんですか？ 必要なときまでポケットに入れておきますよ！」。

　警官は黙った。おそらくガイジンの生活の謎をなんとか理解しようとしているのだろう。それから報告書の記入を続けた。「通常はポケットに入れておき...」。

　次に 登場するのはエドである。彼は地下鉄でかばんをなくした。今回報告書を書いているのは駅長だ。ここでのトラブルの種はエドがかばんを別の物と取り違えていたことである。

　　駅長：「わかりました。あなたは花瓶をなくしたんですね。何色でしたか？」。

　　エド：「黒一色です」。

　神様の次に大切なものは海賊デス

me fill out a report and I'm sure it'll turn up. Now, where did you see your uniform last?"

"With my things on the beach."

The cop pencils on the form, repeating after Andy: "On the beach...Now what kind of uniform was it?"

What kind?? "Um...brown and all leather."

" Brown and all lea..." The cop stops. He eyeballs Andy from his desk. "What do you do with an all leather uniform?!"

Now Andy grows irked. "Well, what do you think I do with it? I carry it in my pocket till I need it!"

The cop pauses, perhaps trying to unravel the mystery of overseas life, then continues writing..."Usually carries in his pocket..."

NEXT comes Ed, who has lost his briefcase on the subway. This time it is the stationmaster writing the report. In this case the vexing words are **kaban**—case—and **kabin**, vase.

kaban
kabin

Stationmaster: "OK, so you lost your vase. What color was it?"

Ed: "All black."

駅長：（書きながら）「どの位の大きさでした？重さは？」。

エド：「そうですね、大体高さが３０センチ、幅が５０センチといったところです。重さは多分５キロかそこらだと思います」。

駅長：（まだ書きながら）「材質は？」。

エド：「硬いプラスチックビニール製です。縁のあたりには金属も使われています」。

駅長：「これは見つかりやすいと思いますよ。こんな花瓶はめったにないですから」。

エド：「いやあ、それを聞いてほっとしました」。

駅長：「ところで、一体なんで花瓶を持っていたんですか？」。

エド：「は？　どこへ出かけるにも、僕はカビンを持って行きますよ」。

駅長：（まゆをひそめて）「しかし、なぜ？」。

エド：「なぜ？　なぜって、大事な書類を入れておくためですよ！　当たり前じゃないですか！」。

神様の次に大切なものは海賊デス

Stationmaster: (writing) "And how big was it? How heavy?"

Ed: "Oh about thirty centimeters high and fifty centimeters wide. Maybe five kilograms or so."

Stationmaster: (still writing) "And what was it made of?"

Ed: "Hard plastic vinyl. With some metal along the edge."

Stationmaster: "I think this should be easy to find. We don't often get items like this."

Ed: "Whew, that's a relief."

Stationmaster: "Why were you carrying it anyway?"

Ed: "Huh? Oh I take my vase everywhere."

Stationmaster: (Knitting his brows) "But why?"

Ed: "Why?? Well, I stick my important papers in it! Of course!"

　　　　　　　　　次の　会話はピエールと職場の同僚との間で
かわされたもの。いま同僚がちょうどピエールに、ペット
を飼っているかと聞いたところである。
　「ここ日本では何も飼っていないよ」ピエールは説明し
た。「僕のアパートは狭すぎるもんだから。でも...」。
　ここで、第一章である買物客がuni（ウニ）の綴りを誤っ
て逆に読んで、inu（犬）と思い込んでいた例を思い出し
ていただきたい。ピエールもこの二語にひっかかった。し
かも、あの買物客とはちょうど逆の勘違いだった。
　「フランスの実家では、ウニを飼ってるよ」。
　その同僚は、フランスといえばエスカルゴぐらいしか
思い付かない人物だったので、ウニをペットにするなんて
風変わりで面白いなと思った。
　「ウニを飼ってるフランス人って多いの？」。
　「うん」ピエールが同僚に答えた。「かなり多いよ」。
　「ウニをどんな所で飼っているわけ？　箱の中？」。
　「違う違う」やれやれ、日本人の中にはずいぶんものを
知らない人間もいるものだと、ピエールはあきれた。
　「兄と僕とで、ウニに小屋を外に作ってやったんだ。鎖
につないでそこで飼っているよ」。
　「鎖に！？」。
　「それはつまり...ウニを放し飼いにするわけにはいか
ないんだよ。近所の人たちがいやがるからね」。

次に　紹介する渡辺繁氏は、アメリカ人の同僚についてまる
で思いもよらなかったようなことを知ることとなる。
　「うわあ...」いま、会社のレセプションで起こり得る
最悪のことが繁にふりかかろうとしていた。会場の隅でロ

神様の次に大切なものは海賊デス

THE next conversation occurs between Pierre and an acquaintance at work, who has just asked if Pierre has any pets.

"Well, not here in Japan," Pierre explains. "My apartment is too small, but...."

Now recall in Chapter One when a shopper reversed the letters for dog and sea urchin — **inu** and **uni**? Here *inu, uni* Pierre takes the same pair of words and twists them back the other way.

"...Back in France my family keeps a sea urchin."

His co-worker, whose knowledge of France stops at buttered escargo, finds this intriguing.

"Do many French do that?"

"Yeah." Pierre tells him. "Quite a few."

"Where do you keep it then? In a box?"

"No, no." Gosh, Pierre thinks, how naive some Japanese are.

"My brothers and I built it a little house outside. We keep it chained up."

"Chained!"

"Well...we can't let it go free. The neighbors wouldn't like it."

NOW we meet Shigeru, who is about to learn something about an American co-worker that he would have never guessed.

"Uh oh..." The worst thing that could happen at these

ジャーにつかまりそうになっているのだ。ロジャーはこの
会社の歴史上——そしてたぶん他のどの会社の歴史におい
ても——もっとも耐えがたい無礼者だった。

　繁はビュッフェの方へすばやく逃げようとした。だが、
手遅れだった。ロジャーの方がすばやかった。

　「よお、渡辺さん」ロジャーは話しかけてきた。「息子さ
んはどう？　今度は試験に合格できた？」。

　「ああ... ロジャーさん... こんにちは」。

　繁が次の言葉を言う前に、ロジャーはもう日本の教育
についてしゃべり出していた。それは、ロジャーが好んで
攻撃的長広舌をふるう話題のひとつだった。繁はその激し
い非難をできるだけうまく身をひいてやりすごした。よう
やく口をはさむ隙ができると、さきほどの質問に答えた。

　「うん、息子は上智大学の入学試験に受かったよ」。

　「上智か」ロジャーは鼻を鳴らして言った。「あそこはお
宅にはちょっと学費が高すぎるね。どうやって払うつもり
なんだ？」。

　「君の言う通り、あそこはちょっと学費が高いようだ。
ぼくはもっと残業に励まざるを得ないだろうな」。繁は儀
礼的に笑みを見せた。彼の心づもりでは、ロジャーにあと
二言ほど言いたいことを言わせてやり、そのあとはトイレ
に逃げ込むつもりだった。

　「おれの忠告を聞きたまえ。一円たりとも払ってはいけ
ない。息子に自分で払わせることだ。そうすることで、息
子は一人前の男に成長するだろうから」。

　これで一言がすんだ。あともう一言聞いてやればいい。
「だけどねえ、働くのも度が過ぎては、勉強ができなくな
るんじゃないかなあ」。

神様の次に大切なものは海賊デス

company receptions was about to occur to Shigeru. He was about to be pinned in the corner by Roger, the most insufferable boor in the history of their office and perhaps of any office.

He tried to scoot to the buffet, but it was too late. Roger had him.

"Well, Watanabe-san," the American began. "How's that boy of yours? Did he pass a test this time?"

"Oh...Roger-san...Hi."

Before he could say more Roger launched into Japanese education, one of his favorite tirades. Shigeru rode the blast the best he could and when he got a chance, at last answered the question.

"Yes, my son passed the exam for Sophia University."

"Sophia," Roger snorted. "That's a bit rich for your blood, isn't it? How you gonna pay for that?"

"Right. I suppose it's a little steep. I guess I'll just have to work more overtime." He laughed politely, planning he would let Roger go on for two more comments, then escape to the men's room.

"Take my advice. Don't pay a single yen. Make the boy pay it himself. It'll make a man of him."

One down, one to go. "Well, if he works too much, he won't be able to study, will he?"

"Nonsense! I did it and it didn't hurt my grades one lick. Yes sir, I didn't take even a dime of my old man's money. I paid my own way through."

Time to sneak away, but before making his excuse,

「ばか言うなよ！ おれ自身、働きながら学んだけど、成績には全然影響なかったぜ。そうとも、おれはおやじからビタ一文だってもらってやしない。自分で働いて、自分で道を切り開いたんだ」。

さあ、今が逃げ時だ。でも、その言い訳をする前に、繁はもうひとつだけロジャーに質問をしたい気分に駆られた。まさにその質問のおかげで、ロジャーの日本語は落とし穴に落ちるのだが。

「どんな仕事をしたの？」。

ロジャーはビールをのどを鳴らして飲み、それからしゃべりだした。「猿洗いさ。それがおれの仕事だった」。

「猿」と「皿」を間違えてることはすぐにわかった。

繁は笑いをこらえた。「猿を、洗ったの？」。

「その通り。週２０時間を４年間続けた。夏には週４０時間も洗ったもんだ」。

「それは大変だったろうなあ」。

「もちろん大変だったさ！ その上給料はショボかったしな。でも、おれは考えたんだ... いまいましいことだが、人間はいつだって清潔な猿が必要なんだ、と。それでおれは猿洗いを続けたというわけさ」。

「きっと...」繁は言うべき言葉をさがすのに苦労した。「猿を洗うのがうまくなったことだろうね」。

「は！」ロジャーは吐き出すように言った。「そりゃあうまくもなるさ！ おれはすごく腕が上がって、数分でカートに山積みの猿をきれいに洗うことができた。だけど、本当のところ...おれはその仕事のおかげでひどい目にあった。つまり、家に帰って手を見ると、お湯に浸して猿を洗うものだから、手がゆでたロブスターみたいに赤くなって

神様の次に大切なものは海賊デス

Shigeru couldn't help but ask one further question. A question that knocked Roger's Japanese for a loop.

"What'd you do?"

Roger slurped down some beer, then yapped, "I washed monkeys, that's what."

The word for monkey in Japanese is **saru** and the word for dishes is **sara**.

saru

sara

Shigeru fought to keep composure. "You washed monkeys?"

"Damned right. Twenty hours a week for four years. Forty hours a week in the summer."

"That must have been hard."

"Of course, it was hard! And it paid like crap, too. But I figured...Hell...people will always need clean monkeys. So I stuck with it."

"You must..." Shigeru struggled to squeeze out his

いるんだ」。

繁は目元の涙をぬぐった。

「何がおかしいんだよ？ 猿洗いなんて下層階級がやるこ
とだって思ってるんだろう？ 猿洗いなんかするのは君の
自尊心が許さないってわけか？」。

「いやいや、そうじゃないよ」繁はロジャーの腕に手を
置いた。「ただ…何て言ったらいいか…白状するけど、ぼ
くは生まれてこの方一度も猿を洗った経験がないんだ」。
そう言うと、繁はもう我慢できなかった。どっと吹き出し
てしまった。「一匹もね！」。

ロジャーは首をふった。「きみたち日本の亭主族は甘や
かされてるな。どうでもいいけど、息子さんが君の二の舞
を演じないようにするがいい。息子にマンガを読むのをや
めさせて、猿洗いをさせろよ！」。

「そうだね... そうだね...」繁は息をきらして言った。
「そうすべきなんだろうね」。

「なんだったら息子さんをおれの所へよこしてくれよ。
そうすれば、猿洗いのやり方を教えてやるから」。

「きみがかい？ 教えてくれるの？ ぜひ頼むよ。それと、
ぼくも行って見せてもらってもいいかい？」。

繁の声に笑いが含まれていることで、ロジャーは何か
が変なのだと気がついた。しかし、それが何であるのかは
わからなかった。この二人の男は互いを見た... 繁の方は
笑いをこらえようとして体がふるえている。ロジャーの方
はと言えば、いつものように背筋をまっすぐ伸ばして立っ
ている。

「失礼」と、ロジャーがちょっとしてから語気鋭く言っ
た。「トイレに行ってくる」。

神様の次に大切なものは海賊デス

sentence. "Have gotten good at it."

"Hah!" Roger spat. "You got that right! I got so good, I could scrub down a whole cart of monkeys in minutes. But I tell ya...the punishment I took. I mean, I'd come home and look at my hands and they'd be as red as boiled lobsters from dipping those monkeys in hot water."

Shigeru brushed a tear from his eye.

"What the hell are you smiling at? You think that's too low class!? You too proud to wash a monkey!?"

"No, no..." Shigeru put a hand on Roger's arm. "It's...just that...Well, I have to admit I've never washed a monkey in my life!" And then he couldn't stop himself. He burst into laughter. "Not even one!"

Roger shook his head. "You Japanese husbands. So spoiled. Whatever you do, don't let the same thing happen to your son. Get his nose out of the comics and get him to washing monkeys!"

"Right...right..." Shigeru wheezed. "I'll have to do that."

"Or send him to my place. I'll show him how it's done!"

"Oh would you? Please? And could I come watch?"

The hilarity in Shigeru's voice tipped Roger that something was wrong. Yet just what he didn't know. The two men faced each other—Shigeru trembling from trying to hold himself together and Roger his usual straight-backed self.

"Excuse me," he snapped after a moment, "I have to go to the men's room."

"Wait!" Shigeru trailed after him. "I'll come with you!

「待ってくれ！」繁はロジャーのあとを追いかけた。「ぼくも一緒に行くよ。猿洗いについてもっと話が聞きたいんだ！　つまり、最初にどこを洗うんだい？　それから、どうやって乾かすんだい？　それから...」。

猿の 次は牛に行こう。

　同じ学校に赴任したばかりの二人の教師——幸子とマージー——は親友になった。それで、夏休みになると、二人は一緒に休暇をすごすことにした。

　二人は車で大阪から九州まで旅行した。その途中あらゆる有名な観光地を見物し、夜は旅館に泊まった。ある日二人の車は、草を食べている牛があちらこちらに見える、阿蘇山の心地よい斜面を走った。その素敵だけれど長かったドライブのあとで、二人は山間の谷間にある田舎風の旅館にやってきた。そこには露天の温泉風呂がついている。

　二人の女性は部屋に直行した。部屋に入ると、マージーは幸子に、浴衣に着替えて、その露天風呂に入ってみようと言った。

　しかし、幸子は車の運転でへとへとに疲れていた。「私にかまわず、お先にどうぞ」と、彼女はあくびをしながら言った。「わたしは横になって休みたい気分なの。温泉にはあとで入るわ」。

　そう言って、幸子は畳の上に布団を敷いて、ひと眠りしようと横になった。そのあいだにマージーは浴衣に着替えて、一人でその温泉を試そうと、足取りも軽く部屋を出て行った。

　一時間もたった頃、幸子はマージーが部屋にもどってきた物音で目をさました。湯上がりの、その若い外国人女

神様の次に大切なものは海賊デス

I want to hear more about washing monkeys! I mean, what part do you do first? Then how do you dry them? And..."

FROM monkeys we move to cows.

New teachers at the same school, Sachiko and Margie have become fast friends. So when summer break rolls around, they decide to vacation together.

The two travel by car from Osaka down to Kyushu, stopping at all the famous sights and staying in ryokans at night. One day after a beautiful, but long drive over the luscious slopes of Mt. Aso, dotted with grazing cattle, the two come to a rustic inn in a fold between hills—an inn with an outdoor hot springs attached.

The two women go straight to their room, where Margie suggests they change into Japanese robes and hit the bath.

Yet, Sachiko is too tuckered from driving. "You go ahead," she yawns. "I just want to lay down and rest. I'll take a bath later."

So saying, she places her bedding on the grassmat floor and curls up for a nap. Margie, meanwhile, changes into a robe and trips off to try the spa by herself.

Almost an hour later Sachiko is awakened by Margie's return. The foreign girl's face shows rosy and fresh from the water, with her red hair slicked and shiny.

"Did you have a good sleep?" she smiles.

性の顔はバラ色で、はつらつとし、その赤毛はつやつやと輝いていた。

「よく眠れた？」と、マージーはほほえみながら言った。

「ええ」と、幸子が答えた。「それでお風呂はどうだった？」。

「すごくよかったわ。ただ...」。

「ただ何なの？」。

「ええと...」マージーはその長い外国人らしい鼻にしわをよせた。

「お風呂に入ったときは、別に何も問題はなかったの。でも、それから振り向いてみると...わたしと一緒にお風呂に入っていたのが何だかわかる？」。

幸子はもう起き上がっていたが、首を横にふった。彼女はマージーの次の言葉を待っている。

「牛がいたのよ！」。

幸子は一瞬息をのんだ。「うそでしょ！？」。

「うそじゃないわ。今まで見たうちではいちばん大きなタイプよ」。

「あなたと一緒にお風呂に入ってたの？」。

「そうよ、ちょうど私の真後ろに」。

「まあ、そんなこと信じられないわ」。

マージーは座った。「そう、わたしもショックだった」。

神様の次に大切なものは海賊デス

"Yes." Sachiko says. "And how was the bath?"

"Oh just great, except..."

"Except what?"

"Well..." Margie wrinkles her long foreign nose.

"When I got in, everything was fine. But then I turned around and...Can you guess what was in the water with me!?"

Sitting up now, Sachiko shakes her head. Margie has her full attention.

"A cow!"

Sachiko gasps. "You're kidding!!"

"Nope. One of the biggest I've ever seen."

"In the water with you!?"

"Yep. Right behind me."

"My gosh! I can't be-lieve it!"

Margie sits down. "Yeah. I was shocked too."

"We have to com-plain!"

"Complain? Nah. It's just life in the country. Nothing to be upset about."

Sachiko is now fully awake. "I don't know how you can be so calm. As for me, I'm not gonna

Japanese Made Funny

「わたしたち苦情を言うべきよ」幸子は言った。

「苦情？ そんな必要ないわ。これが田舎の暮らしってものよ。腹をたてるほどのことじゃないわ」。

幸子は今ではすっかり目がさめていた。「あなたはどうしてそんなに平静でいられるのかしら。わたしならそんなお風呂場に近よる気にさえなれないけど」。

「まあそんなことを言わずに、せめて入ってごらんなさいよ」。

「とんでもない！ 牛となんか一緒にお風呂に入るもんですか」。

「あのねえ、そのことなら心配しなくていいのよ」マージーの顔はとりすました表情になった。「だって、わたし、その牛を殺してしまったんですもの」。

「え？」。

「本当よ。わたし、牛を湯舟から追い出して、そんでプラスチックの腰掛けで打ち殺したの。いい気味だったわ」。

「牛を？」幸子は目をまるくした。「大きい牛を？」。

「すごく大きいやつよ。見たらきっと驚くわよ」。

マージーはそう言ったが、幸子はたぶんさほど驚きはしないだろう。もしマージーが実際に殺したのが、牛ではなく虫だと知ったなら。

のちにマージーは大阪でこれと同じ失態を演じている。窓にとりつける新しい網戸を買いに行ったとき、こう言ってしまった...

「もしこれをとりつけないと、ウシが部屋に飛んで入ってくるんです！」。

神様の次に大切なものは海賊デス

go anywhere near that bath."

"Oh come on! You have to at least try it!"

"No way! I'm not taking a bath with a cow in there."

"Well, you don't have to worry then." Margie's face grows smug. 'Cause I killed it."

"Huh?"

"Yeah. I drove it out of the water and then beat it to death with a plastic stool. Served it right."

"A cow?" Sachiko's eyes moon wide. "A big cow?"

"Real big. You'd be amazed."

But Sachiko might be less amazed if she realized Margie had only killed a **mushi**, or "bug." Drop the "m" *mushi* and one ends up with an entirely different animal, one *ushi* quite a bit larger.

Margie later made the same gaffe up in Osaka when she went to buy new screens for her windows, announcing...

"Because if I don't, the cows fly right in!"

Japanese Made Funny

■■■■■■■　　　　ジュリー　の間違いは、恥ずかしさのランク
がもう少し上の部類に属する。

　ジュリーは就職の面接を受けようと大急ぎだった。
やっと目的のビルを見つけると、ドアをぐいと開けて、息
をきらしながら中に入った... 見ると、目の前に受付の窓
口があった。

　彼女は片手で自分をあおぎ、受付係にほほえみかけた。
その若い受付嬢もジュリーにほほえみを返した。

　「すみませんが」ジュリーは受付嬢に言った。「わたしは
１１時にメンスがあります。どちらに行けばよろしいで
しょうか？」。

　ジュリーは「メンス」ではなく「面接」と言いたかった
のだが…。

　受付嬢の目に心配そうな表情がうかんだ。身をのりだ
して、廊下を指し示した。そして小声で言った。「あの角
まで行って、それから左に曲がって下さい。そこにありま
すから」。

　ジュリーはウインクでお礼を示し、廊下を足早に歩い
て行った。だが、左に曲がって、彼女がそこに見たものは、
女性用トイレだった。それで、彼女はきびすを返して、受
付の方へもどった。

　「すみませんが」と、彼女はまた言った。「わたしのメン
スは１１時きっかりに始まるんです！」。壁にかけられた
時計は１０時５７分をさしていた。「お願いですから、ど
こへ行ったらいいか教えて下さい！」。

　受付嬢は困ってしまった。他の業務ができない。みんな
が自分とジュリーを見ている。

　「ふだんは」と、受付嬢がさらに声を落としてささやい

JULIE'S mistake ranks as a bit more embarrassing.

Rushing to meet a job interview, Julie at last finds the right building, tugs open the door and huffs inside—to find a reception window before her.

She fans herself and smiles at the receptionist, who smiles back.

"Excuse me," she tells the young lady. "But I have an interview at eleven. Where should I go?"

The Japanese word for "interview" is **mensetsu** and the word Julie uses sounds similar—**mensu**—but the meaning is quite different, with the receptionist hearing:

mensetsu
mensu

"Excuse me. But I have my period at eleven. Where should I go?"

The mistake is made more believable by Japanese grammar, which has no articles, like "an" and often drops pronouns like "my."

The young woman's eyes grow anxious. She leans forward, points down the hallway and whispers, "Go to the corner and turn left. The place is there."

Julie winks a thank you and clips down the hall. But when she turns left, all she finds is the ladies' room. So she swings back to the reception desk.

"Excuse me," she says again. "But my period is at eleven sharp!" The clock on the wall reads 10:57. "Please tell me where to go!"

The receptionist is troubled. All work in the office behind her stops. Everyone is watching her and Julie.

た。「わたしたちはこの廊下を行って、左に曲がります」。

　この女性は頭がおかしいんだわ。ジュリーはそう判断した。「おわかりじゃないようですが、私はメンスがあるんです！」。彼女はその言葉を、それぞれの音節を区切ってはっきり発音した。「メ・ン・ス。11時ちょうどに。さあ、わたしはどこに行けばいいのですか？」。

　受付嬢は返答に窮した。おそらく彼女は、外国人女性がこれほどまでに自分自身の生理現象に正確であり得ることに唖然としていたにちがいない。

　ジュリーはこの受付嬢を通さずに何とかやってみようとした。「ねえ、いいですか、田中さんとお話できますか？わたしのメンスは田中さんの担当です」。

　「田中さん？」。

　「そうです。田中さんなしではできないんです」。

　これを聞いて、隣にいた別の受付嬢が事態を理解した。気取らない日本語で、それを表す正しい言葉が難局に直面している受付嬢に伝えられた。またたく間に彼女の顔から不安そうな表情が消え、今では笑いをこらえている表情に変わっている。だが、ジュリーはまるで蚊帳の外で、それにもう10時59分だ。

　「わたしのメンスには、田中さんが必要なんです！今すぐに！」。

　「わかりました」受付嬢は受話器をとり、二桁の内線番号を押した。彼女の両手、唇がふるえていた。

　「ロビーにお客様がいらっしゃいます」と、彼女は受話器に向かって話し、それからその受話器をもどした。「田中はまもなくこちらに参ります」と、彼女はジュリーに言い、田中さんを待った。その姿勢も正しく、まじめくさっ

"Usually," the girl whispers even lower, "We go down the hall and to the left."

This girl is daft, Julie decides. "You don't understand. I'm having my period!" She articulates the word. "P-e-r-i-o-d. Right at eleven. Now where do I go?"

The girl doesn't know how to answer, perhaps dumbfounded that foreign women could be so precise with their biology.

Julie tries to work past the girl. "Listen. Can I speak with Mr. Tanaka? My period is with him."

"Mr. Tanaka??"

"Right. Without Mr. Tanaka, I can't do it."

Now one of the other workers understands. In low Japanese, the correct word is passed up front. In a twinkling, the receptionist's face changes from one of apprehension to one of laugh-control.

But Julie is not in on the joke. And it is now 10:59!

た顔をしていたが、今にも吹きこぼれそうな鍋のように、体がゆれている。彼女の背後にいる社員たちも、同様の表情をしていた。

　ちょうどそのとき、田中さんが階段を足音をたてて降りてきた。彼は一礼して自己紹介した。それからジュリーを階段吹き抜けの方へ案内した。彼女が階段をのぼり、姿が見えなった途端、受付嬢と背後の女性たちがかん高い声で笑うのが聞こえた。

　ジュリーはまだわからなかった...その面接がすんで、女性社員たちがみな立って、微笑をうかべてさようならを言ったときでさえも。

　あとでジュリーは、日本人の夫に受付嬢とのやりとりを繰り返ししてみせたが、このときようやく彼女は自分の踏んだドジを理解できたのである。

　さて、その就職の件はどうなったろうか？田中さんとの面接は大変うまくいき、もう一度会いたいという連絡をもらった。しかしながら、ジュリーはその頃にはもうきまり悪くて、とても出かける勇気などなかった。

　本章の最後に、いちばん恥ずかしいドジを紹介しよう。

　　　　　　　　「彼」と「カレー」は発音がまぎらわしい。「彼」は、文脈によっては「ボーイフレンド、恋人」も意味する。「カレー」は黄褐色で粘り気のあるかけ汁で、日本人はライスにかけて食べるのを好む。

　あいにく、多くの外国人は、この二つの言葉をその違いがわかるように正しく発音するのが苦手である。

　シェリーと美絵は職場の同僚で、いつも昼食を一緒に

神様の次に大切なものは海賊デス

"I need Mr. Tanaka for my period! Right now!"

"Certainly!" the girl takes a phone and punches a two-digit number, her hands and lips quivering.

"You have a guest in the lobby," she speaks into the phone and then sets down the receiver. "He'll be right here," she tells Julie, then waits with her posture erect and her face tight but jiggling like a pot about to bubble over. The office workers behind her look the same.

Just then Mr. Tanaka thumps down the stairs. He bows his introduction and ushers Julie to the stairwell. As soon as she rises out of sight, Julie hears the receptionist and the women behind her shriek with laughter.

She still doesn't get it—even when the interview is finished and the office ladies all stand to smile good-bye.

It is only when she later repeats what she had said to her Japanese husband that Julie understands.

And the job? The "interview" with Mr. Tanaka went so well that Julie was invited to return for a second meeting. Yet by then she was too embarrassed to attend.

LAST, then, we have the most embarrassing blooper of all.

The Japanese words **kare** and **kare** differ in two ways, meaning and pronunciation. The first word is the pronoun for "he." In the proper context this can also mean "boyfriend." The second word means, "curry," especially the thick brown topping Japanese like to ladle

kare, kare

食べる親しい間柄である。二人の会話は唯一の話題を軸に永遠の回転を続けていた。唯一の話題とはすなわち「男」である。

　美絵の場合、彼女の決まったボーイフレンドが話題の中心となる。シェリーの場合はといえば、彼女が夢中になっている男性について、二人はくすくす笑いながら語り合うのが常だった。シェリーはまだその男性とはデートをしたことがなかった。彼はあまりにもシャイすぎて、彼女をデートに誘えないようなのである。

　それで、シェリーはついに自分でコトを進めることにした。彼女はそのはにかみ屋の男性を自宅の夕食に招待した。日時は土曜日の晩と決まった。

　その土曜日の夕方、美絵が自分のデートの用意で忙しくしているとき、電話がなった。シェリーからだった。息をきらし、かなり動揺している様子である。

　「美絵？ あなたのアドバイスが必要なの。お願い、助けて！」。

　「そりゃあ助けるのはいいけど。一体どうしたの？」。

　「わたしって、こういうことがまるでだめなの」。シェリーは息をきらして言った。「昔から苦手なのよ。他の女性はうまいみたいだけど、わたしはだめ。それでも、今度だけは失敗したくないの」。

　「大丈夫、大丈夫よ、落ち着いて。それで、どういうことなの？」。

　「どういうって... つまりその、どうやってあなたは彼を固くするの？」。

　電話で聞くその言葉は、二通りの意味にとれる。美絵は判断に迷った。

神様の次に大切なものは海賊デス

over rice. The latter syllable of this second **kare** is drawn out a bit longer than in the first word.

Unfortunately, many foreigners have rotten pronunciation.

Shelly and Mie were co-workers and regular lunch-time friends, with the conversation forever revolving around a single topic: men.

In the case of Mie, they would talk about her steady boyfriend and when it came to Shelly they would giggle about the fellow she was hot for—a guy she had yet to date. A guy seemingly too shy to ask her out.

So finally Shelly took things in her own hands. She invited the bashful man to her house for supper, the date being set for Saturday night.

Early that evening Mie was busy preparing for her own date when the phone rang. It was Shelly, sounding out of breath and more than a bit agitated.

"Mie? I need your advice. Please help!"

"Well, of course. What is it?"

"I'm just no good at things like this," Shelly panted. "I never have been. Other girls are, but not me. And this time I don't want to fail."

"OK, OK. Slow down. And what is it?"

"How...how do you make your boyfriend hard?"

Mie did a double take at the phone.

"I've been trying and trying for almost an hour and nothing works! Nothing at all! I don't know what I'm doing wrong!"

「もうかれこれ一時間近くいろいろやってみてるんだけれど、どれも効果がないの。まるでだめなのよ。自分のやり方のどこがまずいのかわからないのよ」。

美絵は口を開けた。が、言うべき言葉が見つからなかった。

「美絵、あなたはこういうことが得意だわ。わたしはちゃんと知っているんだから。だから、わたしを助けてちょうだい。時間があまりないの。わたしはこのチャンスを無駄にしたくないの！」。

「シェリー、わたし... 本当に、知らないのよ」。

「とにかく、いいからあなたのやり方を教えてちょうだい。そうしたら、わたしはそれをそっくりまねるから」。

「でも... わたしは知らないのよ」。

「美絵、あなたってわたしの友達じゃなかったの？ 簡単なアドバイスさえしてくれないの？」。

美絵は息をのみ、せかせかと歩き始めた。「まったく、ガイジンったら！」と、髪の毛をかきむしりながら彼女は考えた。こんな個人的なことにまで、いつもいやになるぐらいあけっぴろげなんだから！

「わかったわ、いいわよ... それで、今までどんなことをやってみたの？」。

「ああ、もう全部よ。この種の本は全部買って、そこに書いてあることは全部その通りにやってみたの。でも、どれも役に立たないのよ」。

「全然固くならないの？」

「全然」。

「ちょっと教えてくれる？」美絵は顔がほてってくるのを感じた。「今あなたは何を着ているの？」。

神様の次に大切なものは海賊デス

Mie opened her mouth, but could think of nothing to say.

"Mie, you're good at this. I know you are. So please help me! I don't have much time. And I don't want to lose this chance!"

"Shelly, I...Really, I don't know..."

"Just tell me what you do and I'll do the exact same thing!"

"But...I don't know."

"Mie! Aren't you're my friend! Can't you just give some simple advice?"

Mie swallowed a breath and began to pace. "**Gaijin**!" she thought, clawing a hand through her hair. "Always so damned open about such personal matters."

"OK, OK...So what have you tried so far?"

"Oh everything! I've got all these books and have followed all the directions, but nothing works."

"It's not hard at all?"

"Not at all!"

"Tell me," Mie felt her face grow hot. "What are you wearing?"

Shelly paused. "What the heck does that have to do with it!?"

"Calm down now. It might have a lot to do with it."

"I'm wearing an apron...what do you think I'm wearing?"

"Get rid of the apron then. Get rid of everything you've got on."

　　シェリーは一瞬黙った。「一体全体それが、これとどういう関係があるの？」。

　　「まあ、落ち着いてよ。おおいに関係があるかもしれないのよ」。

　　「わたしはエプロンをつけてるけど... あなたはわたしが何を着ていると思っていたの？」。

　　「じゃあ、そのエプロンを脱いで。身につけているものは全部脱ぐのよ」。

　　「... そうすれば、かたくなるの？」。

　　「ええ、そのはずよ」。

　　「美絵、あなた酔ってるの？」。

　　「わたしの助けが欲しいの？ それとも欲しくないの？」。

　　「あなたはわたしに、着ているものを脱げ、と言ってるのね？」。

　　「そうよ。そして、次は... 今度のはちょっと難しいかもしれないけれど、効くはずよ。わたしの言うことを信じて... ここでは口紅を用意して欲しいんだけど」。

　　「口紅？」。

　　「もしあれば、真っ赤なのを用意してちょうだい」。

　　「美絵、口紅がカレーペーストを作るのとどういう関係があるわけ？」。

　　美絵は凍りついた。カレーペースト！？

　　「彼がそろそろやってくる頃なのに、まだかたくならないのよ」と、シェリーは言った。

　　美絵は口に手をあてた。彼女の目は風船のように大きくなった。

　　「美絵、わたしもう着ているものはすっかり脱いじゃったわ。さあ、次はどうするの？」。

神様の次に大切なものは海賊デス

"...And that will make it hard?"

"It should, yes."

"Mie, have you been drinking?"

"Do you want my help or not!?"

"You want me to take off my clothes?"

"Right. And the next part...Now this might be a bit difficult, but it will work, believe me....For the next part you should get some lipstick."

Japanese Made Funny

　それに答えず黙ったまま美絵は、忍び足で壁にある電話のプラグの差し込み口の方へもどって行った。
　「それで口紅だけど…美絵？　口紅をどうすればいいか教えてよ！」。
　その壁ぎわにきたとき、美絵は電話ごしにシェリーの家のドアのブザーが鳴るのを聞いた。知ーらない、そう思って、美絵はそっと受話器を置いた。
　しかしながら、噂によれば、シェリーとそのデートの相手はうまくいったそうである。

神様の次に大切なものは海賊デス

"Lipstick!"

"Bright red if you've got any."

"Mie, what does this have to do with making curry paste!?"

Mie froze. Curry paste??

"He's gonna be here any minute and I can't get the stuff to harden!"

Mie covered her mouth. Her eyes grew like balloons.

"Mie?? I've got my clothes off now. What's next?"

Silently Mie tip-toed back to the phone jack on the wall.

"And the lipstick...Mie?? Tell me what to do!"

In the background Mie heard Shelly's doorbell ring. Her cue to gently set down the phone.

Word is, however, that Shelly and her date got along fine.

「子象のちんぽ」
分類しようのない言い間違い

　　　　　　　　現実を直視しよう。言い間違いは本当は
何ものにも属してはいないのだ。

　言い間違いはまったくのドジ、へま、しくじり、失
態、ぴかぴかのリンゴの虫食い穴、鏡のひび、魅惑的
なグラビアアイドルの鼻の上の真っ赤なにきびなのだ。

　このように、まさに定義そのものによって、言い間違
いはどこにも拠り所のない落ちこぼれなのである。言い
間違いはどこにも納まらない。要するに、言い誤りの中
には本書のどの分類にも当てはまらないものがある。

　以下に収めた言い間違いの場合、整理しようにもあ
まりに雑然としていてどう分類しようもないか、ある
いは別個に一章をもうけるには、同種の話の数が足り
なかった。聞き違いによるものがある一方、読み違い
によるものもある。また、言い間違いのもっとも強力
な誘発要因によるもの -- つまり推測の誤りによるドジ
-- も含まれる。

　これから紹介する種々様々な言い間違いは、不発
だったり、的を外れたりもする散発的なボトルロケッ
トだ。四方八方に飛んでいくけれど、どれもまったく
同じ場所に落下する。すなわち、言い間違いの国に。

THE LITTLE ELEPHANT'S PENIS

Bloopers from here, there and beyond

LET'S face it. Bloopers don't belong.

For what is a blooper but a boner, a bungle, a bobble, a blunder, a wormhole in a shiny apple, a crack in a mirror, a bright red zit on the nose of a seductive Miss March.

Thus, by very definition, bloopers are outcasts. They don't fit anywhere.

Some don't even fit the divisions of this book!

For the goof-ups enclosed below either defied all attempts at order or as a body of boo-boos totaled too few in number to merit their own separate heading. Some have to do with hearing glitches. Others are related to reading burps. Still others are propelled by the most powerful blooper engine of all—malfunctions in reasoning.

Following, then, come some miscellaneous misfires, sporadic, off-the-mark bottle rockets that spin every which way but always end up dropping in the exact same place—Blooperland.

　　　　　たとえば、アメリカから日本にやってきたば
かりのこの子犬のようにうぶでものを知らない青年の場合
が良い例だ。日本語学校が始まるまでにまだ二週間あり、
彼は自分のアパートを片付けたり、近所を歩き回ったりし
て、時間をすごした。どこへ行っても、「いらっしゃい！」
という言葉を彼は耳にした。ああ、これはきっと「hello!」
を意味するにちがいない、と彼は推測した。日本人とはな
んて友好的な国民なんだろう！

　そんなわけで、この若き社交家は「いらっしゃい！」を
「ハロー！」のつもりで使い始めた。通りで会う人たち、公
園で遊んでいる子供たち、そしてバスの運賃を支払う際に
は運転手にも大声で叫んだ。「いらっしゃい！」。かかって
きた電話にも彼は元気よく応えた。「いらっしゃい！」。

　彼が店に立ち寄り、店員が「いらっしゃい」と言われる
たびに、彼は言葉を返した。「いらっしゃい！」。陽気な性
格そのままに、にこにこ笑いながら。

　近所の人たちは思った。「すごいわ... 今度のガイジン
さんは、アホよ」。

アホな 外国人の話なら他にもある。サムは近所のスー
パーの愛想のいいレジの女の子に惹かれていた。というの
も、彼女は行くと必ずわざわざ彼の様子を聞いてくれるの
だ。「元気ですか？」と、いつも声をかけてくれる。

　「ぼくの国ではどうしてこんな風に気にかけてもらえな
いんだろう？」と、サムは思った。

　毎日サムはその若い女性が担当しているレジに並んだ。
毎日彼女はたずねた。「元気ですか？」。毎日彼は同じ答え

神様の次に大切なものは海賊デス

TAKE, for example, this puppy dog foreigner just off the plane from the States. With two weeks to go before the start of language school, he spends his time sprucing up his apartment and exploring his neighborhood. Everywhere he goes, he hears the word "**irasshai**!"   *irasshai*

Ah, this must mean "hello!" he deduces. How friendly!

Actually, **irasshai** is the word for "welcome." Shopkeepers and restaurateurs call out "**irasshai**" when greeting customers.

Yet, our Mr. Gregarious begins to use it as "Hello." He calls "**irasshai**!" to people he sees on the streets, to children he watches playing in the park and to the bus driver when he pays for his ride. He even answers his telephone with a hearty "**irasshai**!"

When he pokes into a store and the clerk beckons "**irasshai**," he echoes back the exact same word, grinning like the happy fellow he is.

With most locals thinking, "Great...The new foreigner is an idiot."

HERE'S another idiot foreigner story, once again courtesy of *Mangajin* magazine.

Sam is smitten with the cheery check-out clerk at his local store, for she always takes time to ask how he is—this in Japanese being, **Genki desu ka**?   *genki*

"Why don't I get attention like this back home?" Sam wonders.

Each day he lines up in the girl's aisle. Each day she

を恥ずかしそうに言った。「はい、元気です」。

　この淡い恋物語の結末をだれが予想できたろうか。サムはある日知ってしまった。彼女が言ってるのは「元気ですか？」ではなく、「現金ですか？」であることを。

　恥ずかしさのあまり、サムはそれ以来別のレジに並ぶことにした。

　　　　　　恥といえば、試しにリチャードのドジも見てみよう。

　教会での日曜日の礼拝のあと、リチャードは立ち上がって深刻な発表をした。

　「ぼくはこのところずっと胃の具合がよくなくて、昨日医者に行ってきました」。リチャードの唇はふるえていた。

　「... 医者はカンサーについて話しました」。リチャードは cancer（癌）をカタカナ英語で言った。

　会衆ははっと息を詰めた。リチャードはまだ若く、３０前である。それに健康そのもののように見えた。

　「ぼくは明日帰国しなければなりません。どうか... 皆さん... ぼくのために祈って下さい」。

　会衆はその通りに祈った...ただちに。会衆の代表と牧

asks, "**Genki desu ka**?" Each day Sam gives the same shy answer, "**Hai. Genki desu**." "Yes. I am fine."

Who knows where this might have eventually led—except Sam then learned what the girl was really saying.

Not "**Genki desu ka**?" but "**Genkin desu ka**?" Or, *genkin* "Will that be cash?"

Leaving him humiliated enough to choose a different aisle.

SPEAKING of humiliation, try Richard's blooper for size.

After the Sunday service at his church, he stood to make a somber announcement.

"Recently I've had some stomach problems, so yesterday I went to the doctor." Now Richard's lips were quivering.

"...And he talked about cancer." Richard used the Romanized version of the word—**kansâ**.   *kansâ*

The congregation gasped. Richard was young, not yet 30, and seemed in the pink of health.

"I have to go back tomorrow. Please...everyone...pray for me!"

師の二人が、治癒と激励の感動的な祈祷を指揮した。心配でたまらず、牧師はさらに別の措置をとった。

　礼拝のあとで、牧師はリチャードが訪れたクリニックの名前を見つけ、電話をした。

　「昨日きた外国人の方のことですか？」と、医者が答えた。「もちろん、覚えてますよ。あの患者さんは消化不良を起こしていました。わたしは薬を出して、心配しないようにと申しました。でももしそれで患者さんの気が休まるのなら、明日また来院して総合的な検査を受けて下さってもいいと考えました。そのことを伝えましたら、患者さんはひどく落胆した様子でした。ですから、もし気分がいいようでしたら、もう来る必要はないと言っておいて下さい」。

　「検査」という日本語は「カンサー」と発音が似てはいるが、決して生命にかかわるようなことではない。

　リチャードはずいぶんきまりの悪い思いをしたが、祈りがこれほど早く功を奏したのを見たことがないとも告白した。

CANCER に対応する日本語は通常「ガン」であり、operation に相当する日本語は「手術」である。ところが、ビリーにとって「ガン」や「手術」は、別の意味を持つ言葉として聞こえた。

　ビリーは日本語が苦手というわけではない。半年の間に、彼はすでに日本語を母親や父親よりも上手に話せるようになっていた。しかし、ビリーの日本語はまだ十分にう

神様の次に大切なものは海賊デス

They did just that—on the spot. Both the president of the congregation and pastor led emotional prayers of healing and support. Full of concern, the pastor went one step further.

When the service ended, he discovered the name of the clinic Richard had visited and made a phone call.

"The foreigner who came in yesterday?" answered the doctor. "Sure, I remember. He had indigestion. I gave him some medicine and told him not to worry. Yet, if it would ease his mind, he could come back tomorrow for a full checkup. He seemed pretty depressed when I said that, so tell him if he feels better he doesn't have to come."

With the Japanese word for checkup being...**kensa**. *kensa* Close to **kansa**, but not nearly as deadly.

While Richard's embarrassment cut deep, he also admitted he had never seen prayer work so quickly.

THE regular Japanese term for cancer is **gan,** with the *gan* word for operation being **shujutsu**. But these words held *shujutsu* other meanings for Billy.

Not that Billy's Japanese was bad. In six months, he could already speak the language better than his mom and dad. His Japanese just wasn't good enough.

For example, here is his breathless translation of an

まくはなかった。

　たとえば、ビリーは立ち聞きで聞いた近所に住む二人の会話を、次のように息せき切って伝えている。

　「お母さん！ お父さん！ お米屋さんのあのおじいちゃんを知ってる？ あの人、銃で撃たれて死んじゃったよ！」。

　確かにその不運な老人は亡くなっていた。しかし、「銃」（gun）も「撃たれて」（shot）も、ビリーの自己流の解釈にすぎない。真実は、その老人はガンの手術に失敗して亡くなったのである。ガンが銃で、手術がshotとは…。

　「何ということだ、この通りのすぐ先じゃないか！」と、ビリーの両親は考えた。日本は安全な所だと、今まで聞いていたのに！

　この話にはまだ先がある。その米屋の主人の葬式で、ビリーの父親は日本語の決まり文句である「ご愁傷さま」と言うつもりで、未亡人に向かって一礼をした。ところが、彼は早口で言ってしまった。「ゴチソウサマ」。

同様 に恥ずかしい思いをしたのは、自分の息子の葬式を祝うために友人を招待したある婦人である。「わたしたち夫婦は息子が学業を修了したことをたいへん誇りに思っております！」と、彼女は招待状に書いた。「葬式のあと、息子はヨーロッパを旅行する予定です。そして４月からは商社で働き始めます」。

　息子の前途を自慢する気なら、彼女は「葬式」ではなく、正しく「卒業式」と言うべきだった。

神様の次に大切なものは海賊デス

eavesdropped conversation between two neighbors.

"Mom! Dad! You know that old man at the rice shop? He got shot with a gun and died!"

Yes, the unfortunate man had indeed passed away. But "gun" and "shot" had been liberal plugs for **gan** and **shujutsu**.

"My gosh, that's just down the street!" thought Billy's parents. And they had been told Japan was safe!

The story goes on that at the shopkeeper's funeral, the father bowed to the widow with the intention of offering the set Japanese greeting of **Goshûshôsama**, which means "My condolences."

goshûshôsama

Instead he sputtered, **Gochisôsama**, which means "Thanks for the food."

gochisôsama

ALMOST as embarrassing was the foreign wife who invited several friends to her house to celebrate her son's funeral! For she un-wittingly confused a Chapter One word, **sôshiki**, or "fu-neral," with **sotsugyôshiki**, or "graduation."

sôshiki
sotsugyôshiki

"We are so proud of his achievement!" she wrote. "Af-ter his funeral he plans to travel in Europe and from April will begin work at a trading company."

卒業 とは逆に、メリッサとその幼い息子ケンは、幼稚園に入るための面接を受けようとしている。たかが幼稚園に入るぐらいのことで面接を受けるなんて！ メリッサにはほとんど信じがたいことだった。でも、彼女がよく耳にしていたことだが、いい幼稚園に入ることは、いい小学校に入ることを意味した。そして、それはまたいい中学校に、やがてはいい大学に入ることを意味した。メリッサにとって、それは同意しがたい制度である。

　だから、その幼稚園の面接が心配していたような堅苦しいものでないことがわかったとき、メリッサはほっとした。でも、それもつかの間だった。ひとりの先生がケンにほほえみかけ、それからメリッサにたずねた。「きょうだいは？」

　「キョウダイ？」

　メリッサは、京都大学の略称が京大ということを知っていた。それは日本における一流大学のひとつである。

　「まあ、そんなこと、とんでもありませんわ」と、彼女は強い調子で言った。「わたしはそういう考え方に反対です。この時点では、私たちは幼稚園のことだけを考えたいと思っています。大学のことを心配しなければいけない時期まで、まだたっぷり時間がありますから」。面接官はぽかんとした顔をした。ご兄弟は、と聞くべきだったか…。

神様の次に大切なものは海賊デス

AT the other end of the academic ladder we have Melissa and her little boy, Ken...

An interview just to enter kindergarten! Melissa could hardly believe it. Yet she had often heard getting into the right kindergarten meant entrance into the right grade school, which meant entrance into the right junior high and so on up through college—a system Melissa could not agree with.

So she was relieved when the interview turned out not to be the stuffy affair she feared. That is, until one of the teachers smiled at Ken and asked Melissa, "**Kyôdai wa**?"   *Kyôdai*

"**Kyôdai**?"

Melissa knew that as an abbreviation for Kyoto Daigaku, or Kyoto University, one of Japan's top schools.

"Oh no," she stressed. "I'm against that kind of thinking. Right now we just want to focus on kindergarten. There's plenty of time to worry about college later."

To be met with a blank face. For **kyôdai** has another   *kyôdai*
meaning—siblings. With the question of "**Kyôdai wa**?" more properly rendered as: "Does Ken have brothers and sisters?"

今度は数をめぐる言い間違いである。

ある婦人が洋服を買おうと選んでいると、店員たちは彼女にあれこれとおべっかを使った。店員たちは洋服のスタイルや色などを、ぺちゃくちゃ早口でまくしたてた。その婦人のほうは、さまざまな質問や意見が慌ただしく取り交わされる中で、堂々と自分の主張を押し通した。だが、ひとりの店員がある質問をしたとき、彼女の自信は揺らいだ。その質問とは…「バストはおいくつですか？」。

婦人はその質問の意味が理解できなかった。

「バストはおいくつ？」。

彼女はいぶかしげに目を細めた。彼女はその質問のうちの一語が「乳房」を意味し、もう一方の言葉が「数」を意味することを知っていた。ということは...彼女はためらいながら答えた。

「なぜ？ 二つですよ、もちろん」。

「いくつ」はまた文脈によっては人の年令もさす。ミリアムはこのことを知っていた...そしてその知識が彼女の大失敗の原因となった。

ミリアムの親友がまもなく２５歳の誕生日を祝うことになっている。それで、ミリアムは何か特別なことをして、友達をびっくりさせてやろうと計画した。豪華なデコ

NOW some "number" problems, first once more from *Mangajin* magazine.

In the process of purchasing clothes, a foreign house-wife is being fawned over by store clerks. They jabber on about styles, colors and so on, with our gaijin housewife gallantly holding her own in the rapid crisscross of questions and opinions. Holding her own, that is, till one of the clerks asks, "**Basuto wa oikutsu desu ka**?"   *basuto*

Here **basuto** refers to bosom and **oikutsu** is an honor-   *ikutsu*
ific way to say number or, in this context, size. **Wa** marks the preceding noun as the subject of the sentence and **desu ka** is the copulative verb followed by the question marker. In other words, the clerk was soliciting the housewife's bust measurement.

But our foreign wife did not catch the context.

"**Basuto wa oikutsu**?"

Her eyes tilted. She knew one word in the question meant "breast" and the other "number." So...her hesitant answer was:

"Why...two, of course."

IKUTSU, again in the correct context, can also refer to a person's age. Miriam knew this...and that was her down-fall.

Her best friend would soon be celebrating her 25th birthday, so Miriam planned a special surprise, a gorgeous decoration cake delivered to her friend's door. This

レーションケーキを友達の自宅に届けてもらうことにしよう。そう考えて、ミリアムはあるケーキ屋に近づいていった。ところが、彼女が選んだこの小さなケーキ屋は、今までに外国人のお客を迎えたことがなかった。だから、ミリアムが日本語をかなり上手に話すのを知って、ケーキ屋の店主は喜んだ。ミリアムはその誕生日プレゼント用のケーキについてペラペラと説明した。どのくらいビックリさせる見かけにするか、またそれが友達の誕生日に届けられたとき、その友達がどんなに感動するかなど。ちょうどそのとき、店主はペンと注文用紙を手にして、ミリアムに聞いた。「いくつ？」。

　「２５」と、ミリアムは事実をそのまま告げる平板な口調で言った。

　　彼女は年令を示す接尾辞「歳」を省略した。そして、この気の毒なケーキ屋の主人は、外国人に疑問点をただせるような人物ではなかった。この会話の結末を予測できなかったのは、ただひとりミリアムだけである。言うまでもなく、彼女の友達の方は、まったく思いもかけないすばらしい誕生日プレゼントにあずかることとなった。それは見事なデコレーションケーキだった。それも、彼女の２５年間の人生の一年ごとにたいして１個ずつ...。他方、ミリアムは二度驚かされることになった。一度は何が起きたかを知ったときに。もう一度はケーキ屋からの請求書を受け取ったときに。

in mind, she approached a cake shop.

The tiny shop she chose, however, had never had a foreign customer before.

So the baker was pleased to find Miriam's Japanese so strong. Miriam spouted on about the cake, how marvelous it looked, and how her friend would be so thrilled when it was delivered on her birthday. At that very moment, the baker, pen and order form in hand, asked, "Ikutsu?"

"Twenty-five," said Miriam, matter-of-factly.

She did not tack on the age-marking suffix **sai**. And *sai* who was this poor baker to argue with a foreigner?

The only person on earth not able to foresee the outcome of this conversation was Miriam. Needless to say, her friend received quite a birthday surprise indeed:

A beautiful decoration cake—one for each year of her life.

Miriam, on the other hand, got surprised twice. Once when she learned what happened. Then again when she got the bill.

Japanese Made Funny

マーティもまた誕生日で失敗している。まず、ひとりの学生が彼のところへ別の先生へ贈る誕生日プレゼントのことで相談に来た。その学生がたずねた。「リー先生にはどんな贈り物がいいでしょうか？」。

　マーティはなるべく簡単でお金のかからないようにしてあげたいと思った。「国旗がいい」と、マーティは言った。「国旗がリー先生の好物なんだ」。

　「国旗？」と、学生は言った。いくぶん驚いたようである。

　「そう」と、マーティは言った。「リー先生は国旗が何よりも好きなんだ。きみからもらえたら、彼はきっと大喜びするよ」。

　マーティは言い間違えていた。「国旗」とは「クッキー」のことだったのだ。このミスはたいへん悔やまれる。正しい言葉を伝えていれば、リー先生はこれほど途方に暮れるような誕生日ではなく、もっとごちそうの多い誕生日を迎えることができただろうから。

　学生は国旗を文字どおりの意味にとった。だから、リー先生がその学生からもらった誕生日プレゼントはまさに国旗であった。それは壁掛用の大きな星条旗だった。

神様の次に大切なものは海賊デス

MARTY also ran into trouble with a birthday. In this case, a student dropped by to consult him about a birthday gift for another teacher.

The student asked, "What kind of gift would Mr. Lee like?"

Marty tried to keep things simple and cheap. "Cookies," he said. "Mr. Lee likes cookies." He emphasized the word with Japanese pronunciation, for the Japanese term for cookies has been borrowed directly from the English, minus the final "s."

"**Kokki**!?" said the student, somewhat surprised.   *kokki*

"That's right," Marty assured. "There's nothing Mr. Lee likes more. You give him cookies and he'll be overjoyed."

Too bad, Marty had not used the correct term for cookies, which is **kukkî**. Then Mr. Lee might have had a tastier   *kukkî*
birthday, though one perhaps not so bewildering.

For **kokki** means national flag, and that is just what Mr. Lee got: a wall-sized version of the Stars and Stripes.

一方 キースはケーキやクッキーでは我慢できなかった。彼にとってもっと大事な食べ物はハンバーガーだった。語学力が限られており、日本の食べ物を試すのもこわくて、彼は行けるときにはいつでもマクドナルドで食事をすることで、なかなか異文化に適応できない自分をなぐさめていた。

しかし、キースはマスタードに我慢ができなかった。あるいはケチャップが、あるいはピクルスが、あるいはその他の余計なものが。彼が食べたいのはただひとつ、本物のハンバーガー、つまり何も加えていない昔風のプレーンなハンバーガーであった。

問題は、このことをどうやって店員に伝えるかだ。彼はたいてい、薬味を取り除くことで間に合わせていた。その後、ある午後、彼はいいことを思いついた。なぜもっと早くそのくらいのことを考えつかなかったのだろう？ 彼は公衆電話へあわてて走った。それから、日本に長年住んでいるアメリカ人の友達に電話をかけた。電話に出たのはその友人の年若い娘である。

「お父さんもお母さんも出かけてるけど」と、彼女が説明した。

「それはかまわないんだ、エイミー」と、キースは言った。「きみで大丈夫なんだ。ひとつ教えてほしいんだけれど、plain のことを日本語でなんて言うの？」。

「プレイン？」と、エイミーは聞いた。

「そう、plain」と、キースが答えた。

「プレインは飛行機よ」。エイミーは同じ発音のplaneと解釈したのだ。

「ヒコーキ、ヒコーキ、ヒコーキ...」キースは頭に入る

神様の次に大切なものは海賊デス

KEITH meanwhile, would settle for neither cake nor cookies—as hamburger was more his meat. Limited in language and afraid to sample Japanese food, he fed his lin-
gering culture shock by eating at McDonald's whenever
he could.

Except...he couldn't stand mustard. Or ketchup. Or
pickles. Or anything. All Keith wanted was a plain ol'
regular hamburger.

How to communicate this was the problem. Most days
he just scraped the condiments off. Then one afternoon
he got an idea. Why hadn't he thought of it before?

He rushed to a pay phone and called an American
friend with many years in Japan. The man's young
daughter answered.

"My folks are both out," the girl explained.

"That's OK, Amy," Keith said. "You're just as good.
Tell me—What's the Japanese word for "plain?"

"Plane?" asked Amy.

"Yeah, plain," answered Keith.

"It's '**hikôki**.'"   *hikôki*

"**Hikôki**, **hikôki**, **hikôki**..." Keith repeated the word
till he had it memorized. Then he thanked Amy and hung
up, never explaining why he wanted the word and Amy
never asking.

Then Keith marched straight to the McDonald's
counter, confident that he would at last receive what he
wished. And what did he wish?

He enunciated carefully: "**Hikôki** Hamburger! Please!"

までその単語をくりかえした。それから、彼はエイミーに礼を言うと電話を切った。彼はなぜその言葉を知りたいのかを一度も説明せず、彼女の方でも一度もたずねようとしなかった。

それから、キースはマクドナルドのカウンターへ直行した。やっと食べたい物が食べられると、今や確信していた。それで、彼が何を注文するかというと...

彼は注意深くはっきり発音した。「ヒコーキハンバーガーください！」。

店員は目をまるくしたが、キースはしつこく「ヒコーキハンバーガー」を要求した。なぜなら彼は自分の言い方は正しいと思い込んでいたからである。キースには可哀想だが、ヒコーキマックバーガーはメニューにのっていなかった。キースにできたことは、ぶつくさ文句を言い、かわりにKFCに向かうことだけだった。

他方、ナンシーは文句を言うようなタイプではなかった。彼女は誰にでも優しい言葉をかけるような女性である。とはいえ、話す言葉は普段は英語だけだった。彼女の日本語はまだぎこちなくて、さまざまな状況に対応するのはむずかしかった。彼女の夫の方は語学力に恵まれていたが、たいてい仕事で留守だった。今日も夫は留守である。

電話が鳴った。最初、ナンシーは電話に出るべきかどうか迷った。なにしろ相手の言うことを一言も理解できない

神様の次に大切なものは海賊デス

When the attendant's eyes popped, Keith became insistent. He demanded a "**hikôki** hamburger." For he knew the word was correct.

Alas, McAirplane burgers were not on the menu. All Keith could do was grumble and head to KFC instead.

NANCY, on the other hand, was not the grumbling type. She had a kind word for everyone, yet usually only in English because her stiff Japanese would not stretch very far. Her husband was the one with the language skill, but most days, like today, he was off at work.

The phone rang.

At first, Nancy wondered whether she should even answer. After all, chances were she wouldn't understand

可能性が大いにあるのだから。でも…もしこの電話が重要なものだとしたら、どうなるだろうか？　もし誰かが助けを求めているとしたら？

　彼女は受話器を取った。「もしもし…」と、彼女はか細い声で言った。彼女の限られた日本語の語彙の中で、この電話のあいさつはちゃんと使える言葉のひとつだった。電話の向こうから日本人男性の声が聞こえた。案の定、ナンシーには彼が何を言っているのかまるでちんぷんかんぷんだった。だが、彼の熱心な口調は感じとることができた。何か切迫しているような雰囲気さえある。

　「もう一度言って下さいませんか？　もっとゆっくり」。彼女は日本語で何とか話相手を努めようとした。

　すると、男は話をくりかえしてくれた。さらにまたもう一度くりかえした。それでも、彼女にはまるで理解できなかった。だが、彼女はあきらめようとはしなかった。「わたしは紙と鉛筆をもっています。もう一度本当にゆっくり言って下さい。それを書きとめて、日本人の友達に電話をかけるつもりです。その友達は英語を話しますから」。

　そこで、相手はさらにもう一度話をくりかえした。必要に応じてところどころ小休止を入れたり、復唱してくれる。

　やっとナンシーは書き終えた。彼女はその伝言を一語一語復唱し、それから素早く行動に移った。

　「わたしはこれから友達に電話をします」と、彼女はどもりながら言った。「１５分したらもう一度電話して下さい。いいですね？」。

　大急ぎで彼女はミチコに電話をした。ミチコは日本人の主婦だが、海外で育った。「いいわよ」とミチコは言っ

神様の次に大切なものは海賊デス

a word.

Yet...what if the call was important? What if someone needed help?

She lifted the receiver. "**Moshi moshi**..." she peeped, *moshi moshi* the telephone greeting being one of the best lines in her limited repetoire.

From the other end came the voice of a Japanese man. Sure enough, Nancy had no idea what he was saying. But he seemed earnest...even urgent.

"Could you tell me again? Slower?" she managed.

So again, the man told her—and again. But she just couldn't get it.

Yet now she would not give up. "I have a paper and pencil. Tell me again, real slow. I will write it down and call a Japanese friend. That friend speaks English."

So the caller told her yet again, pausing between phrases and repeating when necessary.

At last, Nancy finished. She recited the message back word for word and then zipped into action.

"I'll telephone my friend," she stammered. "You call back in 15 minutes, OK?"

Hurriedly, she phoned Michiko, a Japanese housewife who had grown up abroad.

"OK," said Michiko. "Read it to me."

So Nancy did. "**Okusan no oppai sawaraseteyo**..."

"Nancy! It was an obscene phone call! That man's a masher!"

And not just any masher, but rather the happiest

た。「わたしにそれを読んでちょうだい」。

それで、ナンシーは書き留めた文章を読んだ。「オクサンノ、オッパイ、サワラセテヨ...」。

「ナンシー！ それは卑猥な電話じゃないの！ その男は変態野郎よ！」。

たしかに。しかし、その男はただのありふれた変態野郎ではない。日本中でいちばん幸せな変態野郎だ。よりによってナンシーに電話をしてきたなんて。彼女はこの類の男たちにとって、願ってもない標的である。文句を言わずに卑猥な台詞を聞いてくれ、しかもそれを書き留めて友達に伝えてくれるなんて…。

もちろん、夫が留守のとき、ナンシーは二度と再び電話に出ようとはしなかった。

マーサ の場合、彼女はもっと直接的な形で恥ずかしい思いをした。電話などではなく、彼女はそのとき相手とじかに向かい合っていたのである。

そもそも彼女はいつも婦人科へ行くのがいやでたまらなかった。初診のときはなおさらである。その上、初めて診てもらう医者とセカンドランゲージの日本語で話さなければならないときは二重に苦痛であった。

とはいえ、今度の新しい医者は紳士的な感じである。白髪まじりで思いやりの深そうなタイプだ。雑談をしてマーサをくつろがせようとしてくれる。

「では、こちらに引っ越して来られたばかりなんですね？」。

神様の次に大切なものは海賊デス

masher in all Japan, having struck—in Nancy—the masher's pot of gold.

Needless to say, when her husband was out, Nancy never answered the phone again.

MARTHA met embarrassment in a more direct manner —face-to-face, not over the phone.

To start, she had always hated trips to the gynecologist, especially first visits. And doubly especially when she had to speak to the unknown doctor in her second language—Japanese.

But this new doctor seemed gentle enough—a gray-haired considerate type who tried to help Martha relax with casual conversation.

"So...you just moved here?"

"Yes. From Kyoto."

"And you've been in Japan how long?"

"Six years."

「はい。京都から移って来ました」。

「日本にはどのくらいお住まいです？」。

「6年間です」。

「食べ物などは大丈夫ですか？」。

「ええ、大丈夫ですわ」。

「では、日本の暮らしにうまくとけこんでいらっしゃるわけですね？」。

「はい、どうにか」。

　それから、医者は肝心な質問をした。その際、彼はある医学用語を使ったのだが、マーサがその言葉を知らないことに気づかなかった。日常よく使われている言葉の中に、その医学用語とまぎらわしいものがあった。意味はまるで違うのだが、音はまったく同じなのである。といえば...

「それで、オリモノの方はどんな具合ですか？」と、彼は聞いた。

「オリモノ、オリモノ、オリモノ...」そうだ、その言葉には聞き覚えがある。どういう意味だったかしら？　彼女はすばやく自分の頭の中の記憶を探った。そして、突然思いついた！「織物」のことね！たしか衣服とかカーペットとか織機とかを指す言葉だったわ。

　それにしても、ちょっと変な質問だわねえ。でもまあ、日本人はいつだって変な質問をしてくるもの。それにこのお医者は世間話をしてるだけみたいだし。

　マーサは医者にほほえみかけ、まばたきした。

「オリモノですか？ええ、オリモノって素敵ですわ」。

　これを聞いて、医者は背筋がピンとのびた。

「といっても、自分ではあまり作ったことがありません。やってみたんですけれど、一度もちゃんとできたこと

"No troubles with the food or anything?"

"No."

"You've adapted well then?"

"I guess so."

Then the doctor asked the key question, using an expression with an everyday homonym, not realizing Martha was unaware of the medical term.

"Now how about **orimono**?" he asked. **Orimono** means "vaginal discharge."   *orimono*

"**Orimono, orimono, orimono**..." Yes, she knew that word. What was it? Quickly Martha sifted through her brain, her eyes raised up to the corners. Then all at once she had it!

Orimono! The word for "weaving!" As in clothing, carpets, looms and so on.

Kind of an odd question, but Japanese, she felt, were forever asking odd questions. And this doctor seemed determined to make small talk.

Martha smiled at him and batted her eyes.

"**Orimono**? Oh I find it adorable."

With this the doctor sat up straight.

"Yet I haven't done much myself. I've tried, but it never comes out right."

The doctor stuck out his neck. "What?"

But now Martha was on a roll.

"However, my grandma could really do it. Why, back home we have some of grandma's **orimono** that we have kept for years. It's just too precious to part with."

がないんです」。

　医者は首を突き出した。「何ですって？」。

　しかしマーサはもう止まらなかった。

　「でもわたしの祖母は本当にオリモノが上手でした。私の実家では、祖母のオリモノの一部を長年保存してあります。手放すのがもったいないんですもの」。

　「オリモノをですか？」と、医者は再びたずねた。

　「でもわたしが今まで目にしたオリモノの中でいちばん素晴らしかったのは」と、彼女は続けた。「京都のあるデパートの展示会で見たオリモノですね。世界中のオリモノが展示されていて、思わず見とれてしまいました」。

　マーサがこのお医者とは相性が良さそうだと思い始めたまさにそのとき、医師はいきなり辞書を引っ張り出して、ページをめくり始めた。彼はマーサにその辞書を渡したが、「下り物」という言葉に下線が引かれてあった。

　彼女は耳がカッと赤くなるのがわかった。そして、このお医者のところへはもう二度と来ないと心に決めた。

　　　マーサ　には少なくとも慰めてくれる夫や友達がいたが、クリスには誰もいなかった。

　クリスの語学力ときたら最低で、そのために友達がなかなかできなかった。日本に長く住んでいれば、状況は変わってくるだろうが、彼は今すぐ友達が欲しいのだった。

　それで、彼はとある居酒屋でひとりさみしくビールを飲んでいた。でも、両の耳はそばだてたまま。もし他の客たちの会話に割り込む機会を見つけたら、彼はすかさずそれにとびつくつもりだった。

　二人の男が隣のテーブルにやって来た。どちらもクリ

"Orimono?" he asked again.

"But the best orimono I've ever seen," she continued, "Was at a department store exhibition in Kyoto. Orimono from all over the world. It was fascinating."

She had just decided she liked this doctor when he grabbed a dictionary and flipped through the pages. He handed her the book with the word "orimono" underlined.

She felt her ears flame hot and decided she would never visit this doctor again for the rest of her life.

AT least Martha had her husband and friends to console her. Chris had no one.

Pinned in by marginal language skills, he struggled making friends. More time in Japan might change that, but Chris wanted friends NOW!

So he sat sipping beer at a Japanese pub, all alone, yet with both ears pricked up. If he could spot a chance to push in with some other guests, he planned to grab it.

Two men slid into the next table, both about Chris's age. They ordered mugs of beer, then spent some time

スと同じくらいの年ごろである。彼らはビールを注文し、
そのあとしばらくすべすべしたプラスティック製のメ
ニューをじっと見ていた。クリスは二人の会話をわきで聞
いていた。二人の男はしゃべり続けている。しかし後ろの
客たちの笑い声のために聞き取りにくかった。最初のうち
クリスは一言も聞き取ることができなかった。しかしやが
て…そう、今はっきり聞こえた。ひとりの男が「ミック
ジャガー」と言ったのが。それからまた聞こえた。今度は
もうひとりの男が言った。「ミックジャガー」。

　なんと、この二人の男はローリングストーンズのこと
を話している！　クリスにとって絶好の機会だった。彼は
これを逃さなかった。

　「ヘイ！」。クリスは手を伸ばして、自分のジョッキを相
手のとカチッと合わせた。「ぼくもミックジャガーが好き
なんですよ！」。

　二人の男はクリスをじっと見た。

　「知ってるでしょ、これ」。クリスはおもむろに歌い出し
た。「♪アイキャンゲッノオ、サアティスファ〜クショ
オン」彼は肩をゆすりながら歌った。

　二人の男はまだクリスをじっと見ていた。クリスはほ
ほえみかけた。そして彼は首を上下に振り始めた。

　「それとか、これはどう？　♪シザホーンキトンク、ホー
ンキトンク、ウィメン！　ギミーギミーギミーザホンキー
トンクガール！」。

　ちょうどその時、ホンキートンクではないガールが現
われた。ウェイトレスだった。クリスは何やら悪い予感が
して、元気がなくなった。二人の男のうちのひとりが、メ
ニューに載っている「肉じゃが」の写真を指でさした。今

神様の次に大切なものは海賊デス

studying the slick plastic menu. Chris listened in.

The men chatted on, with background laughter making it hard to hear. At first, Chris caught nothing. Then...yes, quite distinctly...one man said, "Mick Jagger." Then again, this time from the other man..."Mick Jagger."

My gosh! They were talking about the Rolling Stones! So he seized his opportunity.

"Hey!" He reached over and clacked beer mugs. "I like Mick Jagger too!"

The two men stared at him.

"You know..." Now Chris sang, "I ain't got no ....satis-faction! I ain't got no...satisfaction." He swished his

度は彼の言っていることがクリスにもはっきり聞こえた。

「そう…とりあえず肉じゃが二人前お願いします」。

二人はもうクリスの方を見なくなった。そして、自分の聞き違いに気がつくと、クリスの方でも二人から視線をそらした。残っているビールをがぶがぶ飲み干すと、クリスはあわててレジとドアの方へ駆けていった。まるで転がる石のように...

さて、次に登場するのはあるガイジン夫婦である。この夫婦の失敗もやはりメニューに関係があるのだが、二人がひっかかったのは、カタカナ英語「ランチ」である。二人はこれを読みちがえてしまった。その結果は…。

夫婦がメニューをじっと見ているところへ、ウェイトレスがやってきた。

「ご注文はお決まりでしょうか？」。彼女はボールペンをかちっといわせて、書きとめる用意をした。

「はい」と、夫が言った。「ミックスウンチスペシャルをお願いできますか？　きみは何を頼むんだい？」。

「そうね、わたしはあまりお腹がすいていないの」と、

神様の次に大切なものは海賊デス

shoulders as he mangled the lyrics.

The two men kept staring. Chris smiled, with his eyebrows making A-frames. Now he bobbed his neck.

"Or how about...She's a hooonnk...honky tonk woman! Gimme, gimme, gimme the hony tonk girl!"

Just then a different girl appeared—the waitress—and Chris got the blues.

One of the men pressed a finger to a photo of a meat-and-potato dish on the menu. He spoke words that Chris could now plainly hear.

"Yes...to start we would like two orders of **niku jaga**." *niku jaga* With **niku** being "meat" and **jaga** "potatoes."

They kept their eyes off Chris and, by and by, as Chris sensed his mistake, he withdrew his own eyes as well. He guzzled his remaining beer and—like a rolling stone —tumbled fast for the cash register and the door.

HERE we have a foreign couple about to have their own menu misadventure, this time fuzzing on the **katakana**-ed word for "lunch"—which in the Japanese syllabary for borrowed foreign terms comes out as **ranchi**. Yet, in *ranchi* this case, the foreigners misread the word as **unchi**. And *unchi* you know what that means...

The waitress glides up to the couple as the two gaze at their menus.

"Ready to order?" She clicks her pen.

"Yes," says the man. "Can I have the Mixed Poop Special? And how about you, Dear?"

妻が答えた。「何にしようかしら？ …じゃあ、お子さまウンチにするわ」。

　ウェイトレスは笑いをかろうじて抑えていた、おそらくお客様の言うことは常に正しいのだと考えて。「承知しました」と、彼女は夫婦に答えた。「ご希望のものは何でもおつくり致します」。

　最後に、言い間違いの古典的傑作を紹介することにしよう。

　ケビンはやせこけた大学二年生。日本の家庭にホームステイし、目下日本語を勉強中である。ある日の午後、彼はその家のソファに座って、易しい子供向けの本『子象のさんぽ』をその家の二人の姉妹に読んであげようとしていた。姉妹は二人とも高校生である。

　ケビンの失敗はあるひらがなを読み違えたことから始まった。彼の脳はなぜか「さ」を左右逆に見てしまった。彼は、このひらがなが反対の方を向いている文字だとばかり思いこんで、「ち」と読んだのである。

　そんな次第で、この本の題名「子象のさんぽ」と読むべきところを、ケビンは「子象のちんぽ」と読んでしまった。

　声に出してそう読んだところ、姉妹に爆発的な効果が現れた。二人は笑いころげて息もできないほどだった。ようやく笑いがおさまると、きちんと座り、スカートのしわをのばし、このうっかり者のアメリカ人の兄に淑女ふうにほほえんでみせた。そして、ありがちな展開だが、彼にもう一度読んでくれるよう頼んだ。

　ケビンが自分の間違いに気づくまで、これが数回くりかえされた。だが彼は、言い間違いをしていることはわ

神様の次に大切なものは海賊デス

"Oh I'm not so hungry," the wife answers. "I wonder... Could I just get the Kid's Poop Plate?"

The waitress bites her lip, perhaps thinking the customer is always right. "Certainly," she tells them. "Whatever you wish."

FINALLY, we have this blooper classic, picked from the pages of *The Japan Times*.

Kevin was a raw-boned college sophomore, homestaying with a Japanese family and just learning their language. One afternoon he sat on the family sofa and tried to read a simple children's book—*The Little Elephant's Walk*—for his two high school-aged Japanese sisters.

Kevin's bloop came when he misread one character of **hiragana**. His mind somehow flipped the letter for **sa** and read it as if it were facing the other direction, as if it were the letter for **chi**.

So instead of stating the book title as, "The Little Elephant's Walk," with "walk" being **sampo**, Kevin read **chimpo**—or "The Little Elephant's Penis." *sampo*
chimpo

Hearing this aloud had an explosive effect on his sisters. They laughed so hard they nearly choked to death. Finally they brought themselves under control, sat up straight, smoothed out their skirts, smiled lady-like at their unwitting American brother and—predictably—asked him to read it again.

This was repeated several times before Kevin realized

かったのだが、間違えた言葉の意味を知らなかった。彼は姉妹にその言葉の意味を聞いてみた。二人は今ではもう床をたたいて笑いこけている。彼が日本語で「ちんぽってどういう意味なの？」と質問すると、姉妹たちは大笑いしてアザラシみたいな声をあげた。

　それで…彼は台所に行った。そこでは姉妹の母親が夕食のための野菜をきざんでいた。彼が例の質問をすると母親は、侮辱されたと感じた人が示すような反応を示した。ちょうどその時、娘たちが台所に入ってきて、ぺちくちゃとしゃべり、事の次第を母親に伝えた。あっけにとられて黙っていた母親の表情は、苦笑から満面の笑みへ、やがてこらえきれない大爆笑に変わった。

　ケビンは台所のドアをあけた。「もしみんながぼくにこの言葉の意味を教えてくれないのなら」と彼は脅迫した。「道路でこの言葉を大声で叫んでやる！」。母親と娘たちは涙の跡のついた目で互いをじっと見つめていたが、それからまた再びどっと笑い出した。

　ケビンは自分の脅迫を実行した。「ちんぽ！　ちんぽ！」と外でくりかえし叫んだ。その間、母親と娘たちは脇腹をおさえながら、台所をはねまわっていた。

　幸運なことに、姉妹には弟がいた。その弟が帰宅すると、ケビンは例の質問を彼にぶつけてみた。弟はその答えを指でさし示して教えてくれた。

　この話の教訓は、言葉で上手に表現できなくても、場合によっては、適切な身ぶりや手ぶりだけでも十分に意志疎通がはかれるということだ。特に、健全な身体をもっている場合には。

神様の次に大切なものは海賊デス

his mistake. Yet, though he knew he was saying the wrong word, he didn't know what it meant. He tried asking his sisters, who by now were pounding the floor in convulsions. His Japanese question, "What does 'penis' mean?" made them howl and bark like seals.

So...he went into the kitchen where his homestay mom was chopping up vegetables for supper. She reacted to the "P" question the way most people react to a slap. Just then her daughters crawled into the kitchen and managed to babble the little elephant story. Mom went from stunned silence to a wry smile to a big grin to loud, uncontrollable whoops.

Kevin opened the kitchen door. "If you don't tell me what this word means," he threatened, "I'm going to scream it down the street!" The women exchanged tear-streaked glances...and then once again burst into snorts.

So Kevin did it. He repeatedly screamed "penis!" out the door, while his homestay family bucked around the kitchen clutching their ribs.

Fortunately Kevin also had a small homestay brother who came home and pointed out the answer to Kevin's question.

Which shows that when words fail, sometimes all one needs is the right body language—especially if you have the right body.

終わりなき言い
間違いのパレード
そして言い間違いの行進は続いている！

██████████ スージー は不信感に陥っている大家の山田
さんに再び電話をかけた。

「山田さんですか？ 手伝っていただきたいことがあるん
ですけれど。私のお尻にねずみがいるんです！」。

お次はジャックだ。日本でできずに物足りなく思って
いることが他にもある。それについて彼は語る。

「ぼくは柔らかいクソの原であお向けに寝ころんで、そ
して雲が流れていくのを眺めていたいんだ」。

ロジャーはかつて自分がやったアルバイトについて、
さらに詳しく説明する。

「もちろんおれはずいぶん猿を割ってしまったさ。で
も、たいていの猿は接着剤でくっついて、ちゃんと元通り
になったもんだ」。

そして、マージーはさらに多くの牛を殺した。

神様の次に大切なものは海賊デス

THE NEVER ENDING BLOOPER PARADE
And the bloops keep marching in!

ONCE again Suzie calls an incredulous Mr. Yamada:

"Mr. Yamada? I need your help! I've got a mouse in my butt!"

Next Jack tells of another moment he misses:

"I like to lie on my back in a field of soft poop and watch the clouds roll by."

Roger fills in more details on his part-time job:

"Sure, I broke my share of monkeys. But most glued right back together."

And Margie kills even more cows.

"This last one I had to chase all over my house. Finally I cornered it in the kitchen and clobbered it with a slipper."

　「最後の牛ときたら、私は家中を追いかけ回さなければいけなかったの。とうとう台所に追い詰めて、スリッパでめった打ちにしてやったわ！」。

　外国人たちが日本語を曲解し続ける限り、この愉快な失敗のパレードは決して終わることはあるまい。このパレードの太鼓がいちばん大きな音で鳴るのは、常に未来の失敗によってであろう。

　結論として言えることは、語学を学んでいる者は決して言い間違いの国に別れを告げることはできないということだ。たとえできたとしても、それはとりあえず翌日までの別れに過ぎない。

　そのときまでにせめて、読者のみなさんが言い間違いの最高傑作だけに出会われることを祈る。

　そしてみなさんが失敗について聞く側であって、それをやらかす側に回らないことも祈りたい。

For—as long as visitors continue to flex their Japanese—the parade of happy flub-ups will never end, with the biggest bangs on the drum always being those that are yet to come.

In conclusion, language learners never say farewell to Blooperland—only adieu until tomorrow.

Until that time then, may you be visited only by the best of bloopers.

Those being the ones you hear about...not the ones you make.

VOCABULARY LIST

Entries are listed alphabetically with the Japanese word (in Romaji), their English equivalent and the page number on which they first appear.

神様の次に大切なものは海賊デス

神様の次に大切なものは海賊デス

言い間違い募集中

外国人のおもしろい言い間違いを募集しています。
本書の続編で投稿を採用させていただいた方には、
掲載書一冊を献呈致します。

送り先
〒 106-0044 東京
都港区東麻布３－２－１
狸穴アークビル１階
TEL 03-3224-3754
FAX 03-3224-3754
株式会社ザー・イースト・パブリケイション
編集部小林宛
cobayasi@theeast.co.jp

Send us your bloopers

Readers whose bloopers are used in the sequel
to **Japanese Made Funny** will receive
a copy of the new book gratis.

THE EAST PUBLICATIONS, INC.
Mamiana Arc Bldg., 1F, 2-1 Higashi-Azabu 3
Minato-ku, Tokyo

Fax 81-3-3224-3754
sabin@theeast.co.jp